W9-BTH-187

EYE ON
Art

ART DECO

by Diane Yancey

LUCENT BOOKS
A part of Gale, Cengage Learning

GALE
CENGAGE Learning

Detroit • New York • San Francisco • New Haven, Conn • Waterville, Maine • London

© 2011 Gale, Cengage Learning

LIBRARY OF CONGRESS CATALOGING-IN-PUBLICATION DATA

Yancey, Diane.
   Art deco / by Diane Yancey.
      p. cm. -- (Eye on art)
   Includes bibliographical references and index.
   ISBN 978-1-4205-0340-1 (hardcover)
   1. Art deco. I. Title.
   N6494.A7Y36 2010
   709.04'012--dc22

                                                    2010032961

Lucent Books
27500 Drake Rd.
Farmington Hills, MI 48331

ISBN-13: 978-1-4205-0340-1
ISBN-10: 1-4205-0340-5

Printed by Bang Printing, Brainerd, MN, 1st Ptg., 12/2010
Printed in the United States of America
1 2 3 4 5 6 7 14 13 12 11 10

CONTENTS

Foreword

"Art has no other purpose than to brush aside . . . everything that veils reality from us in order to bring us face to face with reality itself."

—French philosopher Henri-Louis Bergson

Some thirty-one thousand years ago, early humans painted strikingly sophisticated images of horses, bison, rhinoceroses, bears, and other animals on the walls of a cave in southern France. The meaning of these elaborate pictures is unknown, although some experts speculate that they held ceremonial significance. Regardless of their intended purpose, the Chauvet-Pont-d'Arc cave paintings represent some of the first known expressions of the artistic impulse.

From the Paleolithic era to the present day, human beings have continued to create works of visual art. Artists have developed painting, drawing, sculpture, engraving, and many other techniques to produce visual representations of landscapes, the human form, religious and historical events, and countless other subjects. The artistic impulse also finds expression in glass, jewelry, and new forms inspired by new technology. Indeed, judging by humanity's prolific artistic output throughout history, one must conclude that the compulsion to produce art is an inherent aspect of being human, and the results are among humanity's greatest cultural achievements: masterpieces such as the architectural marvels of ancient Greece, Michelangelo's perfectly rendered statue *David*, Vincent van Gogh's visionary painting *Starry Night*, and endless other treasures.

The creative impulse serves many purposes for society. At its most basic level, art is a form of entertainment or the means for a satisfying or pleasant aesthetic experience. But art's true power lies not in its potential to entertain and delight but in its ability to enlighten, to reveal the truth, and by doing so to uplift the human spirit and transform the human race.

One of the primary functions of art has been to serve religion. For most of Western history, for example, artists were paid by the church to produce works with religious themes and subjects. Art was thus a tool to help human beings transcend mundane, secular reality and achieve spiritual enlightenment. One of the best-known, and largest-scale, examples of Christian religious art is the Sistine Chapel in the Vatican in Rome. In 1508 Pope Julius II commissioned Italian Renaissance artist Michelangelo to paint the chapel's vaulted ceiling, an area of 640 square yards (535 sq. m). Michelangelo spent four years on scaffolding, his neck craned, creating a panoramic fresco of some three hundred human figures. His paintings depict Old Testament prophets and heroes, sibyls of Greek mythology, and nine scenes from the book of Genesis, including the Creation of Adam, the Fall of Adam and Eve from the Garden of Eden, and the Flood. The ceiling of the Sistine Chapel is considered one of the greatest works of Western art and has inspired the awe of countless Christian pilgrims and other religious seekers. As eighteenth-century German poet and author Johann Wolfgang von Goethe wrote, "Until you have seen this Sistine Chapel, you can have no adequate conception of what man is capable of."

In addition to inspiring religious fervor, art can serve as a force for social change. Artists are among the visionaries of any culture. As such, they often perceive injustice and wrongdoing and confront others by reflecting what they see in their work. One classic example of art as social commentary was created in May 1937, during the brutal Spanish civil war. On May 1 Spanish artist Pablo Picasso learned of the recent attack on the small Basque village of Guernica by German airplanes allied with fascist forces led by Francisco Franco. The German pilots had used the village for target practice, a three-hour bombing that killed sixteen hundred civilians. Picasso, living in Paris, channeled his outrage over the massacre into his painting *Guernica,* a black, white, and gray mural that depicts dismembered animals and fractured human figures whose faces are contorted in agonized expressions. Initially, critics and the public condemned the painting as an incoherent hodgepodge, but the work soon came to be seen as a powerful antiwar statement and remains an iconic symbol of the violence and terror that dominated world events during the remainder of the twentieth century.

The impulse to create art—whether painting animals with crude pigments on a cave wall, sculpting a human form from marble, or commemorating human tragedy in a mural—thus serves many purposes. It offers an entertaining diversion, nourishes the imagination and the spirit, decorates and beautifies the world, and chronicles the age. But underlying all these functions is the desire to reveal that which is obscure—to illuminate, clarify, and perhaps ennoble. As Picasso himself stated, "The purpose of art is washing the dust of daily life off our souls."

The Eye on Art series is intended to assist readers in understanding the various roles of art in society. Each volume offers an in-depth exploration of a major artistic movement, medium, figure, or profession. All books in the series are beautifully illustrated with full-color photographs and diagrams. Riveting narrative, clear technical explanation, informative sidebars, fully documented quotes, a bibliography, and a thorough index all provide excellent starting points for research and discussion. With these features, the Eye on Art series is a useful introduction to the world of art—a world that can offer both insight and inspiration.

Introduction

"Soaring Off into the Clouds"

New York's art deco skyscrapers are some of the most awe-inspiring attractions to be found in the world. Art deco is a decorative movement that was popular in the 1920s and 1930s and influenced the style and decoration of everything from jewelry to steamships. The ever-changing style is hard to define because it reflects the individual viewpoints of its many creators. Nevertheless, it can be identified by its geometric shapes, its elaborate decoration, and its functionality—it was created to be used.

Skyscrapers are the largest examples of art deco design. Their impressive height, angularity, and practicality perfectly express the style. Two of the tallest, grandest, and best-known are the majestic Empire State Building and the silver-spired Chrysler Building. In the 1920s and 1930s when they were first built, these buildings were noteworthy for their tall, pointed towers, their grand lobbies, and the number of businesses they could hold. The two were remarkable for more than their shape and size, however. They were the stars of a colossal building competition that expressed the spirit of the times and of art deco style itself.

An Expression of Wealth and Power

As with all art deco artists, New York designer William Van Alen did not try to conform to a certain look when he set out to design the Chrysler Building in 1927. However, his creation became a perfect example of the style—modern, geometic, highly ornamented, and controversial. It also incorporated what would become a typical art deco theme—the automobile. Author Ron Chernow says, "It was a time when the car claimed the American imagination, and it was land transport soaring off into the clouds."[1]

The building was constructed using the private funds of Walter Chrysler, one of the chief industrialists of the age. Chrysler built cars, and public demand for automobiles helped him earn a fortune. By 1928 Chrysler was rich enough to afford a business headquarters in New York City that reflected

A GROUPING OF TOWERS

Americans, particularly New Yorkers, loved skyscrapers in the 1920s. Although the buildings blocked the sun, they were modern and impressive, as author John Tauranac explains.

By the 1920s, the skyline [of New York] had replaced the Statue of Liberty as the symbol of the city. New Yorkers pointed to the skyline as their pride and joy. . . . No other city had such a skyline, and no other citizen could puff up his chest the same way a New Yorker could. [Author] H.G. Wells described the New York skyline as "the strangest crown that ever a city wore," and architect William F. Lamb, one of the architects of the Empire State Building, declared that "New York's beauty lies in the amazing grouping of its towers."

John Tauranac, *The Empire State Building*. New York: Scribner, 1995, p. 49.

his wealth and power. He wanted it large and attention-grabbing. A new skyscraper, the Bank of Manhattan Trust Building (now the Trump Building) at 40 Wall Street was being built at the time, and its owner claimed that it would be the tallest in the world when finished. Chrysler could not have that—he wanted that title for his own. So, working with Van Alen, he set out to realize his dream.

Van Alen understood the kind of statement Chrysler wanted to make. He decided to create a building that would not only be tall but would proclaim the glory of Chrysler cars. Its pointed dome would be covered with a new kind of shiny metal—stainless steel—with unusual triangular windows that would look like the sun's rays. The building would also be ornamented with huge replicas of Chrysler hubcaps, enormous metal-winged radiator caps, and large metal eagles—replicas of 1929 Chrysler hood ornaments.

Chrysler's Pretty Toy

Ground was broken at the building site on Forty-second Street and Lexington Avenue on September 19, 1928. Just over a year later, in October 1929, both the Chrysler Building and the Bank of Manhattan Trust Building were nearing completion. Getting into the spirit of the competition, builders on the Wall Street project had increased the height of their building from sixty-eight to seventy-one stories, which they were sure would top the Chrysler Building.

They reckoned without Van Alen's creativeness, however. The designer had secretly built a seven-story steel needle to set atop the skyscraper's dome. One night, when no onlooker could see, he and a crew of men hauled it up a central elevator shaft and put it in place. The next morning, everyone was treated to the new addition that had suddenly made the building taller than the one on Wall Street. Architecture critic George S. Chappell declared, "It is distinctly a stunt design, evolved to make the man in the street look up. It has no significance as a serious design."[2]

Stunt or not, when the building was completed on May 28, 1930, the addition allowed Chrysler to take credit for having

Completed in 1930, New York City's Chrysler Building was America's first art deco skyscraper.

the tallest building in the world. More important, the stainless steel dome on his building reflected the sun like a mirror and called attention to itself from miles away. Van Alen called it his "fire tower." Journalists called it "Chrysler's Pretty Bauble

[toy]" and "Manhattan's Mightiest 'Minaret [tower].'" Chrysler himself was more matter-of-fact. "[It is] a bold structure, declaring the glories of the modern age,"[3] he said.

Another Competitor

Even though Chrysler and Van Alen had outwitted their competitors at 40 Wall Street, the record they held for world's tallest building was short-lived. Work had already begun on the Empire State Building, designed by American architect William F. Lamb and owned by a group of businesspeople headed by another automobile maker, John J. Raskob of General Motors. Groundbreaking had taken place on January 22, 1930, and with a labor force of thousands, the building rose at a record four and a half floors per week.

Like the Chrysler Building, the Empire State Building was art deco in style. Built during the Great Depression, it was less decorative than the flamboyant Chrysler Building, but it was still ultramodern, geometric, and highly ornamented. Metal mullions (columns) ran between the windows and ended in floral design caps. Its windows were separated by aluminum spandrels, or reinforcements. Aluminum had not been used on building exteriors prior to that time.

At street level, stone eagles sat atop columns beside the front entrance. Sleek stainless steel canopies ran above entrances on Thirty-third and Thirty-fourth streets. The front entrance led into a grand lobby lined with multicolored marble and granite. The lobby's walls were decorated with large bronze medallions and a metal mosaic of the exterior of the building. Its ceiling was covered with aluminum, platinum, and gold leaf stars and circles.

Sweeping the World

The top of the Empire State Building was not as showy as that of the Chrysler Building, but it was equally art deco, made of new types of materials, and crafted along geometric lines. The designers had created an aluminum, steel alloy, and glass mast, which jutted upward like a needle into the sky. From the base of the mast, angular metal wings rose upward and outward.

DAY AND NIGHT

The Empire State Building and the Chrysler Building are both breathtaking examples of art deco architecture. Their looks highlight the fact that the style was complex and sometimes contradictory, as author Ron Chernow explains.

I've always been torn as to which is my favorite skyscraper, the Empire State or the Chrysler Building. It's a hard decision, because the Empire State has this elegant poise and majestic air of calm and beauty. The Chrysler Building has a different silhouette. It's jazzy and electric and jagged, the beautiful but brash cousin. The Empire State Building expresses the daytime personality of the city: power and business. The Chrysler Building appeals to the night, to the fantasy life of the city in its glitz and glamour.

Quoted in Elaine Louie, "How It Sparkled in the Skyline," *New York Times*, May 26, 2005, p. F8.

The New York City skyline at dusk with the Chrysler Building on the left and the Empire State Building on the right.

Art deco was intended to be functional, and so was the mast. In a decision that illustrated the forward-looking spirit of both the era and the style, designers built a mooring pole at the top of the mast. This was intended to be a docking site for dirigibles, huge metal airships that were a popular form of transportation after World War I. The plan did not work, but the mast and pole remained a gleaming capstone that made the building the tallest in the world.

The height of the Chrysler and Empire State buildings attracted attention in the 1920s and 1930s, but their architecture and decorative features are what made them showpieces

"I'M NEW!"

William Van Alen, the designer of the Chrysler Building, was born in 1882 in New York City. He attended Pratt Institute, a private art college in Brooklyn, and in 1908 won a scholarship to the prestigious École des Beaux-Arts (School of Fine Arts) in Paris. Excited at the thought of modern design, he stated upon graduation: "No old stuff for me. . . . I'm new! Avanti [forward]!"

Back in New York in 1920, Van Alen's designs received mixed reviews. "Van Alen's stuff is so darned clever that I don't know whether to admire it or hate it," said architect Richard Haviland Smythe. It was not until 1928 that the young designer achieved renown by creating the Chrysler Building. Although recognized for his work, he had to sue Chrysler for his fee after its completion. Chrysler, in turn, accused him of taking bribes from subcontractors.

The incident permanently tarnished Van Alen's reputation. He designed more buildings but never recovered his former glory. He is not even mentioned in Chrysler's autobiography, written in 1937, and upon Van Alen's death in 1954 the *New York Times* did not run his obituary.

Quoted in Neal Bascomb, "For the Architect, a Height Never Again to Be Scaled," *New York Times*, May 26, 2005, p. F10.

through the years. Other skyscrapers have been built that are taller, but none display so well the art deco style. Author and enthusiast Mary Frank Gaston observes, "Art deco often is described not only by such words as chic, clever, elegant, smart, sophisticated, streamlined, and tailored, but also as amusing, flippant, risque [naughty], and fun!"[4]

The style also expressed to perfection the spirit of the 1920s. The times were restless, fast-paced, and rebellious, and art deco gave them expression. Decorative art expert Fiona Gallagher writes, "The . . . style, which swept across the world in the 1920s and 1930s . . . reflected an advancing society that shook off the cobwebs of the previous century and embraced the twentieth century with a vigor that still vibrates today."[5]

1

A Fast and Frantic Era

Art deco arose in the 1920s, developed and changed throughout the 1930s, and came to an end in the 1940s. It was modern—its creators wanted to leave old styles behind and look to the future. In fact, it was called style moderne, or modernistic style, throughout the era. It was also decorative, intended to be applied to useful objects. Architects, graphic artists, glassmakers, interior decorators, movie set designers, and automobile designers incorporated it into their work. As a result of the many who independently expressed their vision of what "modern" looked like, it was considered by some to be a hodgepodge of looks. Some people liked it; others did not. But all agreed that it was extremely diverse and hard to categorize.

Diverse and Contradictory

In fact, the style was often contradictory. The Chrysler Building demonstrated its highly ornamental aspect. The buildings of New York's Rockefeller Center, on the other hand, showed that it could be stark and clean. Susie Cooper's pottery was brightly colored, while Depressionware dishes were delicate and pastel. It could be as playful as a neon-lighted theater marquee (entrance), or as vaguely disturbing as one of Tamara de Lempicka's sultry portraits. In general, however, it was identified by its geometric quality and stylized designs. Stylization is the style an artist uses, and art deco stylization tended toward simplified figures that gave off a feeling of movement, energy, and athleticism. Author John J.G. Blumenson writes, "Art deco is characterized by a linear, hard edge or angular composition, often with a vertical emphasis, and highlighted with stylized decoration."[6]

Although art deco is diverse, two motifs (distinctive forms or figures) repeatedly appear in the artists' designs. The first is the sunburst—a central disk with lines or spires radiating from it in the manner of the sun's rays—which made its first appearance at the 1925 Paris Exposition. There, the front façade of the Galeries Lafayette department store pavilion was decorated with a huge sunburst design. The second form is the fountain, and again, the first one was seen at the Paris Exposition. Glassmaker René Lalique's 45-foot crystal fountain (13.7m), *Les Sources de France*, stood at the entrance of the exhibition and was the grandest of many fountains on the grounds. Designers used the two motifs more subtly, too, as with the crown detail and the stylized fountain of clouds behind the enormous raised figure entitled *Wisdom* on the GE Building in New York City.

Pictured are examples of the two basic motifs used in art deco: (left) the sunburst design at the Galeries Lafayette department store and (right) René Lalique's crystal fountain *Les Sources de France*.

Art deco can also be identified by certain repetitive themes. Those themes include edgy pastimes like smoking, drinking, and dancing; women and the female form; physical activities including sports, driving cars, and flying airplanes; consumerism; and early and foreign cultures. In the 1920s these were the popular interests of modern society, especially the younger generation. Youth was disillusioned with the past, ready to rebel against old traditions. Young people were eager for a style that incorporated and expressed their new attitudes and interests in fearless, unconventional ways. Art expert Dan Klein writes, "The century before the Second World War saw perhaps the most radical changes ever to take place in the history of design."[7]

Bitterness and Disappointment

Much of the rejection of early traditions that is expressed in art deco style was caused by World War I, which had been fought in Europe between 1914 and 1919. When the bloodshed, suffering, and sacrifice of the war ended, peace seemed like an illusion. The victors squabbled over the terms of the Treaty of Versailles, the peace treaty that ended the war. Germany and its allies were defeated, but resentment festered because they had to pay for the damage they had caused as well as give some of their land to the victors. A Communist-led Russian Revolution sent fears of socialism and totalitarianism through the West.

In the United States, President Warren G. Harding called for a return to "normalcy," but, in fact, many people were tired of government, of the old leadership, and with "doing the right thing." Journalist John F. Carter Jr. wrote in 1920, "We have seen the rottenness and shortcomings of all governments even the best and most stable. . . . We have seen entire social systems overthrown. . . . In short, we have seen the inherent beastliness of the human race."[8]

Many discontented members of the younger generation tried to find new meaning for their lives. They left farms and small towns and went to cities like New York, London, and Berlin, where they could try out different lifestyles. Many young artists and writers went to Paris, which was a hub of culture at the time, to share ideas and express themselves through their art.

They painted pictures that were unrealistic and unrefined and that jarred and confused viewers. They wrote about immorality, disillusionment, and disloyalty. They shocked the world by rejecting God, family, and country. As author F. Scott Fitzgerald put it, "Here was a new generation, grown up to find all wars fought, all Gods dead, and all faith in mankind shaken."[9]

Rebellion

Although not all young people rebelled as dramatically as those who went to Paris, many rejected their parents' way of life. Author Frederick Lewis Allen writes, "They found themselves expected to settle down into the humdrum routine of American life as if nothing had happened, to accept the moral dictates [rules] of elders who seemed to them still to be living in a . . . land of rosy ideals which the war had killed for them. They couldn't do it, and they very disrespectfully said so."[10]

This new generation went to work in the daytime to support themselves, but they also had as much fun as they could at night. They spent their money on the latest in modern clothing. They danced and smoked cigarettes. They stayed out late at nightclubs where daring, sexually explicit entertainment was the rule. They also drank heavily, although Prohibition made it illegal for Americans to do so. In early 1919 the U.S. Congress had passed the Eighteenth Amendment making the sale, manufacture, and transportation of intoxicating liquor illegal throughout the country. In January 1920 the "Noble Experiment" began, and many Americans suddenly realized that they did not like living in a country that did not allow alcohol.

It was not just the younger generation who disagreed with Prohibition. Plenty of older Americans were also willing to break the law rather than change their drinking habits. Unable to buy alcohol legally, they sneaked into illegal nightclubs (known as speakeasies) and drank cocktails made from alcohol smuggled into the country. They brewed beer, wine, and "bathtub gin" in their basements. Even the Speaker of the U.S. House of Representatives, Nicholas Longworth, had his own still (equipment for making liquor). His wife said of her husband, "The idea that people could be

Rebellion was a hallmark of the 1920s, but young people's defiant behavior sometimes caught parents off guard. Author W.O. Saunders gives a personal experience in a 1927 article titled "Me and My Flapper Daughters."

I was sure my girls had never experimented with a hip-pocket flask . . . or smoked cigarettes. My wife entertained the same smug delusion, and was saying something like that out loud at the dinner table one day. And then she began to talk about other girls.

"They tell me that that Purvis girl has cigarette parties at her home," remarked my wife.

She was saying it for the benefit of Elizabeth, who runs somewhat with the Purvis girl. Elizabeth . . . made no reply to her mother, but turning to me, right there at the table, she said: "Dad, let's see your cigarettes."

Without the slightest suspicion of what was forthcoming, I threw Elizabeth my cigarettes. She withdrew a fag [cigarette] from the package, . . . inserted it between her lips, reached over and took my lighted cigarette from my mouth, lit her own cigarette and blew airy rings toward the ceiling.

My wife nearly fell out of her chair, and I might have fallen out of mine if I hadn't been momentarily stunned.

W.O. Saunders, "Me and My Flapper Daughters," *American Magazine*, August 1927, p. 27.

prevented from purchasing alcoholic liquor for use in their own homes seemed to him an intolerable denial of the rights of the individual. He, and many others who felt likewise, did not have the slightest intention of complying with the Eighteenth Amendment and never even pretended to."[11]

A Time for Women

The growing determination of women to play important roles in modern society was reflected in art deco artists' incorporation of modern female styles and interests in their work. In the 1920s young women decided they were no longer going to accept the traditional attitude that females were less capable than men. Before World War I women could not vote. They relied on their husbands or fathers for money. They wore modest dresses, went to church on Sunday, and stayed home to raise their children. When young men went overseas to fight, however, women filled in for them in the fields, factories, and other workplaces. Work gave them a taste for independence, while the Nineteenth Amendment, which became law in 1920, gave them the right to vote.

Filled with a modern and independent spirit, many young women—nicknamed "flappers"—decided that a career was more exciting than marriage and motherhood. Some found work as salespeople. Others opened their own businesses such as beauty shops or tearooms. Some decided to go to college, where they prepared themselves for careers.

To make their appearance match their new attitude, they cut their long hair into bobbed or extra-short shingled styles. They threw away their corsets and petticoats and slipped into sheer stockings and short dresses of flimsy material. They put on dramatic makeup and flashy jewelry. When they went out in the evening to a show or a nightclub, they took their cigarettes and slipped a flask of bootleg alcohol into their purse.

Love Affair with Cars

To get to nightclubs and everywhere else around town, cars were necessities as well as symbols of sophistication and success. They were also part of society's fascination with machines and speed, and art deco artists helped design them and incorporated their shapes into other creations.

Cars became affordable in the 1920s due to newly developed mass-production techniques such as the assembly line. Carmaker Henry Ford had created the first assembly line in Detroit, Michigan, in 1914. On it, cars moved on a conveyer past workers, who each added one part until the car was completed. The process sped up assembly time and allowed for huge reductions in costs to consumers. Other car companies

Hundreds of parked cars near a beach in Massachusetts in 1925 attest to the rising affordability and popularity of the automobile. Mass production had made cars affordable for the average American worker.

like Chrysler and Chevrolet soon copied Ford's assembly line, but they went one step further and made affordable cars in a variety of colors. Ford's original models were available only in black.

By 1927 everyone who could afford a car bought one. Designers tempted their customers with colors and offered two-door phaetons (open cars that seated five), sporty roadsters, sedans, and pickups. In the 1930s cars became even sleeker and faster and were given sophisticated names like Royale, Continental, and Imperial. One 1920s fashion columnist, Grace Margaret Gould, observed, "There is nothing secretive about the motor car. It says, in effect, as it makes its whirling way, 'If you want to see the latest thing out, look at me and look at my passengers.'"[12]

Fitness and Flying

Many art deco designs reflect the public's love of sports in the 1920s and 1930s. Thousands of fans turned out to cheer football star Red Grange, known as the Galloping Ghost, who was named a three-time All American and appeared on the cover of *Time* magazine on October 5, 1925. They admired golfer Bobby Jones, who won thirteen national championships between 1921 and 1930. They idolized George Herman "Babe" Ruth, who transformed the game of baseball, hitting a record sixty home runs in 1927. "No one hit home runs the way Babe did," recalled Dizzy Dean, another baseball great. "They were something special. They were like homing pigeons. The ball would leave the bat, pause briefly, suddenly gain its bearings, then take off for the stands."[13]

In addition to watching sports, more people began taking part in them. For the first time, women were inspired by female athletes like Helen Wills Moody, who captured her first tennis title in Wimbledon in 1927 and, in the words of journalist Robin Finn, became "the first American born woman to achieve international celebrity as an athlete."[14] There was also Suzanne Lenglen of France, who earned the women's singles tennis title at Wimbledon six times between 1919 and 1926 and scandalized the older generation with her sleeveless shirts and short skirts that had not been seen on a tennis court before.

Along with sports, flying was the rage. Airplanes had first been used in combat in World War I, and when pilots returned from war, they supported themselves by "barnstorming"—visiting small towns, showing off their flying skills, and taking paying passengers for rides. Fascinated by the danger and the challenges of soaring through the sky, more people took up the pastime, and flying clubs, like the Ninety-Nines Club for female pilots, were formed. Daring individuals like the club's first president, Amelia Earhart, aimed to set flying records by going farther or faster than anyone else. Earhart, who attempted to fly around the world in 1937, gained international attention, particularly after she disappeared over the Pacific,

This 1939 World's Fair poster is a great example of advertising inspired by the art deco movement.

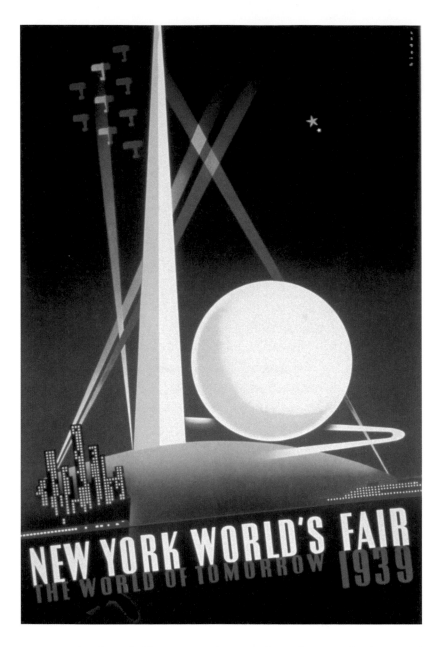

never to be found. Despite such tragedies, flying, which paired advanced technology and speed, captured the public's imagination and was reflected in many art deco designs.

The Modern Consumer

Art deco focused on advanced technology, but it also drew on the prosperity of the 1920s and played on the public's desire to accumulate material goods and live the good life. A 1928 presidential campaign ad declared that President Herbert Hoover had put a "chicken in every pot. And a car in every backyard, to boot."[15] Businesses expanded after the war. There seemed to be jobs for everyone. The stock market soared, and more people became investors and made their fortunes. Banks made housing loans and financed new construction. In fast-developing areas like Los Angeles, California, and Miami, Florida, real estate developers built new homes at top speed, equipping them with state-of-the-art features like electric lights, telephones, flush toilets, and built-in bathtubs.

Families wanted and could afford beautiful furnishings to put in their newly built homes, too. Many of those furnishings were art deco designs—everything from stylish furniture to labor-saving devices like toasters, washing machines, and electric vacuum cleaners. And if money ran short, a new concept, buying on credit, allowed people to take the product home immediately and pay for it in the future. One observer noted, "The rise and spread of the dollar-down-and-so-much-per plan extends credit for virtually everything—homes, $200 overstuffed living-room suites, electric washing machines, automobiles, fur coats, [and] diamond rings."[16]

Art deco designers found a market in the advertising industry, which hyped all there was to buy. Prior to the 1920s, advertising had been low-key. Now it was everywhere, from magazines and newspapers to radios and billboards along highways. More important, advertisements played on the buyers' emotions, persuading them that they needed a product to be happy, attractive, or successful. For instance, a 1920s ad for an early phonograph showed a group of happy children in a garden, clustered around their well-groomed mother. "Fortunate are the children in homes made musical by the Columbia Grafonola,"[17] says the ad.

Converging Cultures

Art deco also reflected the public's interest in a new kind of music that swept the world in the 1920s. That music was jazz. Jazz started in African American nightclubs in New Orleans, Louisiana, and was called the "devil's music" by some who considered it too fast, rhythmic, and passionate. Some white

Americans also disliked jazz because it began as a primarily black musical form, and negative views of African American culture were prevalent. Ann Shaw Faulkner, the president of the General Federation of Women's Clubs and an organizer of a crusade against jazz in 1921, reflected this, stating that "jazz was originally the accompaniment of the voodoo dance, stimulating half-crazed barbarians to the vilest of deeds."[18]

In part because many of their elders considered jazz scandalous, the younger generation loved it. They danced to it in ballrooms and flocked to black nightclubs to enjoy it. Those who lived in Paris made sure to see African American entertainer Josephine Baker, who had gained notoriety for her jazz singing and exotic dance numbers. In time, jazz caught on and was played by black and white musicians throughout the world.

In addition to jazz, art deco was influenced by the Harlem Renaissance—a flowering of African American intellectual life that took place in the 1920s in black neighborhoods such as Harlem in New York City. Between 1914 and 1918, thousands of blacks had migrated from the South to cities like Chicago and New York to look for new opportunities. From their midst, gifted, ambitious authors and academics rose to fame, among them Langston Hughes and Alain Locke. As a result, blacks gained greater visibility in the mainstream community, and whites gained greater appreciation for their culture.

Broadened Horizons

As a result of America's involvement in a war in Europe, Americans gained more interest in world affairs and world trends. They no longer paid attention only to local news. They listened to the radio, went to movies, and stayed up-to-date on national and international events. For instance, when pilot Charles Lindbergh attempted to fly solo across the Atlantic Ocean to Paris in May 1927, millions followed his flight through radio reports. His success made him an international hero and sparked new interest in travel to what were once thought of as far-off places.

Singer Josephine Baker personified the Lost Generation in her reck-lessness and her rejection of traditional American values. Born in St. Louis, Missouri, in 1906, she began performing onstage at the age of fifteen. Outraged by racial discrimination, she moved to Paris in 1925 and gained fame for her funny yet risqué song and dance acts. In one, she performed wearing nothing but a few necklaces and sixteen bananas strung together as a skirt. However, by 1927 she was the most successful American entertainer working in France and was idol-ized as the "Bronze Venus" and the "Black Pearl."

Like art deco style, Baker was versatile. She became a French citi-zen and worked for the French Resistance during World War II. She took part in the early civil rights movement in America in the 1950s, and in 1963 participated in the March on Washington with Martin Luther King Jr.

On April 8, 1975, Baker per-formed for the last time in Paris for an audience that included Princess Grace of Monaco, singer Diana Ross, and actress Sophia Loren. Four days later she died of a stroke—bleeding in the brain. More than twenty thousand people turned out for her funeral proces-sion, and the French government honored her with a twenty-one-gun salute, making her the first Ameri-can woman buried in France with military honors.

The incomparable Josephine Baker performs onstage in the early 1960s.

That new interest was seen in art deco's incorporation of styles from Eastern, Middle Eastern, and Native American cultures. China and Japan had fascinated Americans for decades, but beginning in November 1922, that fascination took second place to a new interest in Egypt. At that time, newspapers reported that archaeologist Howard Carter had discovered boy-pharaoh Tutankhamen's tomb in the Valley of the Kings. In the coming years, reporters and tourists visited the site to try to see the treasures that had been buried for some three thousand years. Descriptions of the mummy and the precious objects found in the untouched inner chamber produced a popular craze known as "Tutmania" and resulted in the use of Egyptian motifs on everything from book bindings to fabric.

Along with interest in ancient Egyptian culture, artists were captivated by discoveries of archaeological remains in North and South America. Archaeologist Earl Halstead Morris began uncovering ruins, first believed to be Aztecan, in the state of New Mexico in 1917. It was later determined that the structures and artifacts were of ancestral Pueblo people, now known as the Anasazi, who lived from the 1100s through 1200s. In Mexico in 1924, archaeologist Sylvanus Morley and others began uncovering impressive Mayan remains that included the pyramids, columns, and carvings created by that civilization in the first century. While the New Mexico ruins were declared a national monument in 1923 to protect the area from tourists, some architects adopted the spirit of the style and made it part of the changing look of art deco in the 1930s.

The Great Depression

Art deco style changed dramatically around 1930, strongly influenced by changes in world affairs that took place at that time. For Americans, economic prosperity ended in 1929. Many who did not have money to spare had borrowed to invest in the rising stock market, and when the price of stocks unexpectedly went down in late October, they lost money they did not have and began to panic. Widespread selling occurred, the stock market crashed, and the economy collapsed. Banks failed, taking millions of people's savings with them. Businesses struggled

BLACK THURSDAY

On October 24, 1929, the rising "bull" stock market that had led to a decade of prosperity in the United States began to fall, ushering in a decade of poverty known as the Great Depression. Historian Frederick Lewis Allen describes the panic that marked the day remembered as Black Thursday.

By eleven o'clock traders on the floor of the Stock Exchange were in a wild scramble to "sell at the market." Long before the lagging ticker could tell what was happening, word had gone out by telephone and telegraph that the bottom was dropping out of things. . . . The leading stocks were going down two, three, and even five points between sales. Down, down, down. . . . Where were the bargain-hunters who were supposed to come to the rescue in times like this? Where were the big operators who had declared that they were still bullish [optimistic]? Where were the powerful bankers who were supposed to be able at any moment to support prices? There seemed to be no support whatever. Down, down, down. The roar of voices which rose from the floor of the Exchange had become a roar of panic.

Frederick Lewis Allen, *Only Yesterday: An Informal History of the 1920s.* 1931. Reprint, New York: Harper and Row, 1997, pp. 247–48.

Anxious people on Wall Street in New York City wait for news as the stock market crashes on Black Thursday, October 24, 1929.

to survive, and many closed. Factories locked their gates. Unemployment soared; in 1933 almost 25 percent of the working population was out of work. Local governments faced great difficulty with collecting taxes to keep services going. Because the United States had economic ties with other countries, the Great Depression, as it was called, spread until it affected the entire industrialized world.

In addition to disastrous economic conditions, troubling international events were on everyone's mind. In 1933 Adolf Hitler was elected chancellor of Germany and began to expand his power. The weak Weimar Republic, which had governed Germany since the end of World War I, gave way to the Third Reich, a nationalist socialist dictatorship led by Hitler. Between 1936 and 1938 in the Union of Soviet Socialist Republics (USSR), dictator Joseph Stalin launched the Great Purge, a campaign to rid the Communist Party of people accused of sabotage or treachery. During the purge he imprisoned, deported, and executed millions, including Americans who had emigrated there to escape the Depression.

Not all the news was bad, however. Prohibition was repealed in 1931. Many construction projects like the Empire State Building that had been started before the stock market crash were completed as planned. New building projects continued, although they were scaled back to save on money. Franklin Delano Roosevelt, who was elected president of the United States in 1932, provided new job opportunities with his Works Progress Administration (WPA), which employed millions in public works projects. As part of the WPA, the Federal Art Project created jobs for American artists, whose work was displayed in public places throughout the nation. Much of that work exhibited art deco style.

Life Goes On

Despite all the economic and international turmoil, art deco lived on, supported in large part by young couples who continued to get married, buy homes, drive their cars, and occasionally go out to the movies. It was the golden age of Hollywood, which had embraced art deco, incorporating the style in its sets, its costumes, and its more than fifty classic films that were made in the 1930s. Everyone loved stars like Clark Gable in *Gone with the Wind*, Judy Garland in *The Wizard of Oz*, and Fred Astaire and Ginger Rogers in *Top Hat* and *Follow the Fleet*.

They also loved art deco style, primarily because it reminded them of better days, gave a promise of hope for the future, and was affordable even if one was poor. The style was versatile, too. It remained modern, even though its creators scaled back its exuberant look to make it less ornamented and more compatible with the times. Decorative art expert Nancy McClelland writes, "[Art deco had] sufficient flexibility to make the transition between the Radio City Music Hall, a Cord 'Phaeton' car, a set piece for a Busby Berkeley film, a juke-box or the Louisiana State Capitol. This same flexibility made it appropriate for the exclusive or the mass-produced without ever losing its identity."[19]

2

Sunbursts, Zigzags, and Color

Art deco had its roots in the early 1900s, when European artists and designers began to rebel against earlier styles. These styles ranged from the somber, cluttered Victorian design of the late 1800s to the turn-of-the-century arts and crafts movement, whose supporters believed that there was no beauty in mass-produced things. Instead, these rebels wanted to move ahead and embrace the advances of the machine age. They wanted to prove they could combine art and craftsmanship to create functional articles that were beautiful, too. Historian Bevis Hillier explains, "Art deco's ultimate aim was to end the old conflict between art and industry, the old snobbish distinction between artist and artisan [craftsperson]."[20]

The Exposition

In 1914, to draw attention to their ideas, several members of the Société des Artistes Décorateurs (Society of Decorative Artists) in Paris began planning for an international trade fair of modern decorative art. The society included architect Hector Guimard, artist Eugène Grasset, potter Raoul Lachenal, architect Paul Bellot, and artist Emile Decoeur. The fair, which they entitled Exposition Internationale des Arts Décoratifs et Industriels Modernes (International

Exposition of Modern Industrial and Decorative Arts), was designed to display the ideas and talents of modern artists, decorators, and craftspeople in everything from architecture to fashion accessories.

The exposition did not take place until eleven years later, due to World War I and a shortage of funds. When it did, however, it attracted contributors from around the world. Countries such as France, England, Greece, Japan, Russia, and others set up huge exhibits or pavilions so they could display the work of their leading artists. Only two major counties did not take part. Germany was not invited because of the strained relations resulting from the war. The United States did not accept its invitation because, according to then secretary of commerce Herbert Hoover, there was "no modern art in the United States."[21]

Visitors, however, found the exposition breathtaking. It was set on the banks of the Seine River, in the heart of Paris. The Eiffel Tower, covered with colored lights, sparkled in the

The pavilion of the Factory of Sèvres at the 1925 Paris International Exposition of Modern Industrial and Decorative Arts was just one of many exhibitions that awed spectators. The exposition was designed to showcase modern decorative art.

distance at night. Tall columns topped with stone fountains and decorative ironwork stood at either side of the main gate. Within the gate, trees and gardens formed lush backdrops for more outdoor art. A 1925 article in *Vogue* magazine observed, "Enormous fountains of glass play among life size cubist trees. . . . Enter the pavilions and . . . you find furniture of startling and unprecedented shape, decoration of every imaginable design on walls, floors and ceilings."[22]

Appealing Architecture, Distinctive Design

Exploring the expo, visitors were delighted by the various pavilions sponsored by major French department stores and countries like Belgium, Sweden, and Czechoslovakia. They exclaimed over the Perfume Pavilion with glass designer Lalique's sparkling perfume bottles and glass fountain. They were shocked by Swiss-French designer Le Corbusier's Pavilion de l'Esprit Nouveau (New Spirit Pavilion), which was almost empty and had a slab of concrete sticking out over a living room scene. They wandered down avenues of boutiques that sold designer products and watched fashion shows that featured the latest designer clothing styles.

Although the United States had not participated in the exhibition, the artwork and designs were so unusual and so captivating that American artists quickly joined in the movement. Their first efforts were sometimes failures, however. American art critic Emily Genauer wrote in 1925, "They turned out a succession of wild 'modernistic' pieces, ugly things that revealed no real understanding on the part of their designers . . . and the results were unfortunate."[23]

Before long, however, Americans grasped the spirit of the style and began creating beautiful art deco work. Especially in the area of architecture, they met and surpassed European designs. The first modern skyscrapers were built in America. So were some of the first modern theaters, railway stations, and municipal buildings, as well as "diners"—mobile home–shaped restaurants covered in stainless steel panels and decorated with multicolor bands of neon tubing. An advertising brochure for one of the leading manufacturers of the era proclaimed, "Jerry O'Mahony dining cars embody more than just the practical equipment for food service. They have an appealing architecture and a distinctive design which is attractive and will remain so throughout the years."[24]

Art Deco's Background

Style moderne, or modernistic style, was the term used for art deco until 1966. Although the style was considered new and fresh, its creators gained some of their inspiration from movements that had come before. One of the most important was art nouveau (new art), which was popular beginning around 1900.

Art nouveau was also decorative; that is, it was applied to architecture, glass, ceramics, and other articles of art. It was characterized by romantic and natural images such as trailing vines, flowers, and beautiful women with long flowing hair and

POPULAR TASTE

The Paris Exposition of 1925 launched the new style moderne and gave it an audience. Not everyone in the audience liked it, however, as author Helen M. Daggett outspokenly wrote in 1935.

Do not think that the style known today as "modernistic" is the thing to buy for your home: the style identified by the sharp, zig-zag lines, the points, angles and garish colors. This style cannot last very long, of course because it will not "fit in" gracefully with other types and periods of furniture. You will see this "modernistic" style in public places like the corner store . . . or in any place where a new fad is used for the purpose of attracting the attention of passers-by. But for use in the house in good taste—No! Such a style does not belong there!

Quoted in Lucy Fischer, *Designing Women.* New York: Columbia University Press, 2003, p. 22.

clothing. It was dominated by graceful lines and had a dreamy quality.

Art deco was like art nouveau in that it was new and could be applied to a variety of objects. Art deco artists, however, took the art nouveau look and made it more angular and edgy. Author Robert Fulford writes, "If Art Nouveau's forms were rounded, Deco's were geometric. . . . If Art Nouveau was cozy, Deco was chic. Art Nouveau loved earth tones, but Deco adored brilliant scarlet, jade, purple or orange. Art Nouveau venerated [respected] individual craftsmanship, but Deco embraced machine-made products, from glassware to fabrics."[25]

Classical Influence

Art deco designers were inspired by other early styles, too. They were familiar with neoclassicism, for instance, which drew upon Western classical art and culture, usually that of

This relief on the RKO Building in New York City shows the neoclassical design that influenced the art deco movement.

ancient Greece and Rome. Neoclassicism grew out of the discovery of ancient Italian artwork at the ruins of the cities of Herculaneum and Pompeii in the mid-1700s. Neoclassical artists and architects liked to incorporate columns, decorative pediments (triangular-shaped areas below the roofline on the end wall of buildings), friezes (bands on the outer part of a building), and figures drawn from ancient Greek mythology into their work. The Lincoln Memorial with its columns and carved friezes, built in the early 1920s in Washington, D.C., is an example of neoclassical design.

Early art deco architecture reflects elements of neoclassical style, particularly the use of repeating columns or vertical elements. As art deco developed, however, designers often simplified or stripped columns down to their essentials. For instance, Charters House, an English country home designed in 1938 for engineer Frank Parkinson, features a group of five tall windows flanked by pillars that reinterprets a classical portico, or porch.

Art deco also borrowed from neoclassical design in its use of sculptural figures, particularly women. Most of this kind of ornamentation, such as the raised circular plaques with female figures depicting "Dance," "Drama," and "Song" on the walls of the RKO Building in New York City, is seen on the exteriors of public buildings. Raised neoclassic figures, such as bronze plaques of nymphs (beautiful maidens from Greek mythology), can also be found on art deco furniture and freestanding figurines such as that of Diana the Huntress, a goddess from Greek mythology.

Asian Influence

Anglo-Japanese style is another early movement that shaped art deco. An awareness and appreciation of Asian designs and culture had arisen in Europe and America in the late 1800s as a result of the opening of Japan to trade with the Western world in 1854. Western artists had been fascinated by the unusual subject matter, techniques, and colors that were used in Asian art and had quickly incorporated those elements into their own designs.

Art deco not only borrowed from other early styles, it benefited from a collaboration of artists on both sides of the Atlantic Ocean. Art enthusiast Richard Whitehouse explains:

*A*rt deco was . . . a product of the fertile artistic exchange between Paris, France, and New York City that occurred after World War I (1914–1918). American artists, writers, and musicians flocked to Paris after the war and brought with them a fresh approach to creative work. The French, who grounded their art in a firm grasp of tradition, absorbed something of the American spirit of improvisation [inventiveness]. Later, American architects who had trained at Paris's École des Beaux Arts (School of Fine Arts) brought European influence to the design of New York's many art deco skyscrapers.

Richard Whitehouse, "Art Nouveau to Art Deco," *Modern Silver*, October/November 2001. www.modern-silver.com/artnouveaudeco.htm.

Art deco artists did the same. They designed using Asian screens, gongs, and incense burners. They incorporated exotic Asian materials such as bamboo, ebony, and jade into their furniture. They added shine to their work using Asian-inspired glazes and lacquers.

Asian motifs cropped up in other pieces, too. Designers made clothing in Chinese silk and created kimono-style dresses and wraps for women. Japanese and Chinese scenes were applied to wallpaper, dishes, and fabric. Cherry blossoms, Buddhas, fans, and peacocks could be found on vases, rugs, and vanity cases.

Avant-Garde Influence

As art deco developed, designers were influenced by artistic styles that were current in the 1920s. Many of these, such as constructivism, cubism, futurism, and fauvism, were avant-garde (experimental or innovative). For instance, constructivism, which originated in Russia around 1919, rejected the idea of "art for art's sake." Its supporters believed that art should serve practical purposes. Art deco artists embraced that idea to create pieces that were useable as well as decorative. As industrial designer Nathan George Horwitt said, "Without use there is no beauty/without beauty—what is the use."[26]

Cubism, another avant-garde style, emphasized geometric shapes. A great deal of art deco was based on those same shapes and images. The Cubist influence can be seen in everything from French artist Sonia Delaunay's patterned carpets to Ukranian-French artist A.M. Cassandre's poster designs of bicyclists, trains, and ships.

The influence of other "isms" can be seen in art deco as well. Both futurism, an Italian art and activism movement that began around 1910, and art deco incorporated images of speed, technology, and youth in their work. Futuristic artists aimed to express what they saw as the energy, violence, and vitality of life, especially as it was embodied in machines. Fauvism, a short-lived movement started in the early 1900s by a group of French artists, and art deco are both characterized by bright colors. Unlike art deco, however, fauvism is purely artistic, characterized by wild brush strokes and highly simplified portrayal of subject matter.

High and Low Deco

As art deco developed, it fell into two loose categories based on quality and price. "High deco" was expensive, out of reach of the average man or woman. It was often produced in France and was sold only on commission or in upscale stores. It was considered mass-produced because more than one of a piece was made, but in reality it was usually hand styled, created by well-known architects, artists, and sculptors, and crafted using expensive materials. Pieces might include gold-covered ivory sculptures, handcrafted tables and chairs, and jewelry encrusted with diamonds. "New creations have never been for the middle classes," said French designer Jacques-Emile Ruhlmann of his work. "They have always been made at the request of an elite which unsparingly gives artists the time and money needed for . . . perfect execution."[27]

As deco grew in popularity, more manufacturers produced it, and it became more affordable. Called "low deco," it was made in large amounts and is generally inferior in quality to higher-end pieces. Art deco glassware made in Czechoslovakia, for instance, is not as delicately made as pieces made by Lalique, and the colors are often muddy rather than clear.

At the time, low or mass-produced deco was found in department stores ranging from Macy's to Sears. While wealthy shoppers scorned such work, the average housewife appreciated it. Although it was crude in comparison to higher-grade pieces, it was much more beautiful or colorful than anything that had been on the market before.

A 1950s dining room table, complete with mass-produced art deco placemats and glassware.

Deco Variations

In addition to quality and affordability, art deco was categorized by three variations that affected its appearance during the twenty years of its popularity. Classic moderne was the first and was most conservative. During the early 1920s, many designers and artists still thought in terms of earlier styles and thus relied on them strongly when creating new deco pieces. For instance, a room might have geometric lines but be furnished with Neoclassical-style furniture. Over time, as the designers experimented with and incorporated different looks, classic moderne became less classic, developing into either zigzag or streamline (smooth and simple) design.

Zigzag moderne was one of the most popular variations of art deco. It earned its name from the stepped pyramid shapes, reminiscent of a set of stairs, that so many deco artists used in their designs. Zigzag moderne relied heavily on geometric, right-angled shapes. Even figures that were normally curved—plants, clouds, or women's long hair, for instance—were made angular. Zigzag moderne can be found on everything from the exterior of buildings like the Empire State Building in New York City and the Niagara Hudson Building in Syracuse, New York, to the ventilator grilles in Radio City Music Hall in New York City. There are subtle examples of it, too, on clocks, in jewelry design, and in textile patterns.

Regional variations of zigzag moderne developed, too. The most prominent is Mayan revival, which is found on buildings primarily in the southwestern United States. The most notable architect to work in the style was American Frank Lloyd Wright. Wright stated, "I remember how as a boy, primitive American architecture stirred my wonder [and] excited my wishful admiration."[28] Wright's Hollyhock House in East Hollywood, California, is classic Mayan revival style. The exterior walls tilt inward at the top, suggesting a pyramid. Its windows are small. Inside, a central courtyard is surrounded by a complex system of split levels and roof terraces. Rows of raised, stylized hollyhocks march along the roofline and appear on walls, columns, planters, and furnishings.

Streamline Moderne

After the Great Depression stalled the economy in the 1930s, few artists and architects could afford to create lavish, highly decorated pieces of art deco. Thus, the style underwent a third modification, which was called streamline moderne. Author Eva Weber explains, "When the party came to an end with the 1929 stock market crash, art deco accordingly downshifted into a more somber and conservative vein."[29]

Streamline moderne style is smooth and sleek. The word *streamline* refers to shaping an object to reduce its resistance to a current of air or water. With streamline moderne, unnecessary sharp angles and elaborate decoration were eliminated, to be replaced with straight or curved, clean lines. The style was applied to the most mundane of objects such as pencil sharpeners, refrigerators, and gas pumps. Most often, however, it was seen on buildings. These were usually built of concrete blocks, which were smoothly covered with stucco instead of bricks and stainless steel. Corners and windows were rounded, and curving chrome was used as an accent. Roofs were flat, and colors were often pastel rather than bright. The Del Rio House in Santa Monica, California, built in 1931 by art director Cedric Gibbons for his wife, Hollywood star Dolores del Rio, is an example of a streamline moderne home.

There are regional variations of streamline moderne, and one of the most colorful of these arose in Miami Beach, Florida, in the 1930s. Known as tropical or nautical deco, it is distinguished by buildings that are streamlined and painted white but decorated with pastel horizontal lines for trim. It also incorporated raised exterior motifs typical of the tropics—flamingos, ocean waves, and palm trees. Author Adrian Tinniswood writes, "Flat roofs, fins, and decorative bands of parallel lines abound. There are . . . nautical rails and streamlined curving bays. Indeed Miami Beach possesses the finest and most cohesive collection of art deco architecture in the world."[30]

Shagreen and Bakelite

Because art deco artists designed everything from buildings to jewelry, the materials they used could range from stone,

THE BERKELEY SHORE

wood, and glass to fabric, paper, paint, metal, and precious stones. They often chose unusual materials to express their visions, however. For instance, some experimented with mottled brown or dyed tortoise shell, produced from the shell of the hawksbill turtle, now an endangered species. Others used eggshells or abalone shell with its pearly, blue-green surface. As an alternative to fabric or leather, shark or stingray skin (known as shagreen) was popular. The skin, which was covered with round, closely set scales, was ground down to give a roughened surface. It was then commonly dyed with green vegetable dye and used to cover books, chair cushions, and even tabletops.

Some art deco artists experimented with unusual wood such as Indonesia's Macassar ebony, which was black and streaked with tan or brown tones. Macassar ebony was highly prized for use in making fine cabinetry. Others turned to new

This hotel in South Beach, Florida, is an example of tropical deco style.

A collection of radios, cigarette lighters, desk clocks, and dice in the art deco style are made from plastics like Bakelite and Catalin.

types of metals such as aluminum or stainless steel, which could be used for everything from decorations on buildings to art deco–inspired flatware (forks, knives, and spoons). Colored glass tile known as Vitrolite was also popular. Designers applied it to everything from storefront facades to the surfaces of art deco bathrooms and kitchens.

A newly developed plastic called Bakelite was used by many art deco designers, too. Created in 1907 by Belgian chemist Leo Baekeland, who was trying to find a replacement for shellac (made from the excretion of lac beetles), the hard synthetic material heralded the beginning of the age of plastics. It came only in drab colors such as brown and black but could be molded into a variety of shapes and was incorporated into hundreds of everyday items such as inexpensive jewelry, radio covers, and appliance handles. Other plastics soon followed Bakelite. One of the most popular was Catalin. It came in a variety of colors and became known as "Bakelite's Gaudy Brother."[31]

Deco Designers

One of the most arresting combinations of materials used in art deco design was chryselephantine—a combination of ivory, bronze, and other metals. The word itself stems from the Greek word *chrysos*, meaning "gold," and *elephantine*, meaning "ivory," and refers to an ancient Greek technique of making statues and figurines by bonding the two materials together. In the 1920s artists like Demetre Chiparus of Romania and Ferdinand Preiss of Germany became famous for their small sculptural pieces of ivory, which they formed in the shape of human figures. They then covered the figures with a thin layer of gold or bronze and decorated them with silver, marble, and onyx. In the 1930s Belgian sculptor Claire Colinet gained renown for her chryselephantine Dancers of the World series, which included *Ankara Dancer*, *Roman Dancer*, *Crimean Dancer*, and *Mexican Dancer*.

In addition to Chiparus, Preiss, and Colinet, dozens of notable art deco designers worked both in America and in other countries during the 1920s and 1930s. American Frank Lloyd Wright made a name for himself in architecture. Tamara de Lempicka was a renowned portrait painter. Russian-born Romain de Tirtoff, also known as Erte, was a master in a range of fields, including fashion, jewelry, graphic arts, and interior design. Kem Weber was a German furniture and industrial designer, an architect, and an art director. In the late 1930s, Weber was the main architect for the art deco–inspired Walt Disney Studios in Burbank, California.

Considering the popularity of art deco, relatively few artists and craftspeople gained fame for the work they created.

Tamara de Lempicka, one of the best-known portrait painters of the art deco period, was born in Warsaw, Poland, in 1886. She began painting at the age of twelve and later studied painting under French artists Maurice Denis and André Lhote.

As an artist, de Lempicka lived an unconventional lifestyle. She was friends with artists Pablo Picasso, Jean Cocteau, and André Gide. She was notorious for the many sexual affairs she had with both men and women. She gained fame for painting society leaders, members of the aristocracy, and movie stars. Her work was characterized by a simple but sultry style and was displayed in the most elite galleries of the day. One of her most renowned pieces is a painting of herself seated in a car, entitled *Tamara in the Green Bugatti*. It captures the period's disillusionment as well as its love of style, cars, and women. A journalist describing the portrait stated, "She is wearing gloves and a helmet. She is inaccessible, a cool disconcerting beauty, behind which a formidable beauty can be glimpsed—this woman is free!"

As she grew older, de Lempicka grew disillusioned with modern art. She moved to Mexico in 1978 and died in her sleep there on March 18, 1980. Unconventional to the end, she directed that her ashes be scattered over the volcano Popocatépetl, south of Mexico City.

Quoted in Gilles Neret, *Tamara de Lempicka, 1898–1980*. Cologne, Ger.: Taschen, 2001, p. 9.

De Lempicka's self-portrait Tamara in the Green Bugatti *captures her love of cars, style, and freedom.*

There was no way that they could. By the 1930s the demand for everything from ashtrays to automobiles was so high that hundreds of decorators were kept busy every day. Experts Bevis Hillier and Stephen Escritt explain, "art deco influenced the appearance of everything from packaging and posters to vehicle design and building."[32] Art deco was a total style, and as such, it touched the lives of everyone from London to Los Angeles, and from Napier, New Zealand, to New York, New York.

3

Deco and the Department Store

Art deco was applied art. That is, it was made to be used, either on its own or as decoration on something functional, such as a bowl or a building. It did not result from artists' lack of interest in fine art—paintings or music that serve no purpose other than beauty. Rather, it stemmed from their unhappiness with poorly made goods that were being created in factories in the early 1900s. They wanted to prove that mass-produced, practical articles could be as beautifully made as any purely artistic masterpiece.

Because such articles needed to appeal to both artistic and practical people, however, they were often criticized. For instance, the average man or woman was likely to see the tall, elongated backs of skyscraper chairs and elegant liquor cabinets mounted on metal skis as ugly and impractical. "Fantasmagoric" (disturbing and fantastic), "incongruous," and "vulgar" were just a few of the terms used by those who did not appreciate the unfamiliar mix of shapes, colors, and ideas.

Some critics rejected the notion that commercial items could be considered fine art. French architect Auguste Perret remarked in 1925, "I would like to know who first stuck together the two words 'art' and 'decorative.' It is a monstrosity."[33]

Others were sure that the style was merely a fad that should not be taken seriously. "The present vogue for new character of detail and ornament will wax and wane without leaving any permanent and valuable contribution to our freedom in design,"[34] said J. Monroe Hewlett, chair of the American Institute of Architects' Committee on Allied Arts.

Be Smart, Be Modern

Because art deco was different from what had gone before, it took some getting used to. Merchandisers, however, were

Art deco artists created advertisements using catchy slogans and dynamic images like this one.

quick to see that they could make money if they sold the public on the notion that everything about it was chic, smart, and necessary for happiness. To that end, they placed persuasive advertisements in newspapers and magazines. One that pushed subscriptions of *Vanity Fair* stated, "Modernism is sweeping the intelligent world. You find it in music, in the arts, in literature. You just can't ignore it. . . . There is a way, an easy way, to know and enjoy the newest schools of modern thought and art. . . . This forum is the magazine *Vanity Fair*."[35]

Art deco graphic and poster artists were hired to create convincing advertisements for everything from soap to vacations. Instead of the factual, wordy ads of previous eras, dynamic images and punchy slogans played on everyone's desire to be attractive, to save time, and to have fun. Designers for alcoholic beverage ads, for instance, used beautiful women to persuade drinkers to buy everything from Martini & Rossi vermouth to Joseph Perrier French champagne.

Dozens of art deco artists who designed ads never became famous. However, many like Aubrey Hammond, Ernest Dryden, Riccio Loris, and Leon Benigni produced beautiful work for many companies. French designer Jean Dupas was widely recognized for his advertisements for Saks Fifth Avenue department store.

Leaders in Advertising

Italian Leonetto Cappiello, known as the "father of modern advertising," was one of the most prolific poster artists of the period. Living in Paris, he created ads for everything from Le Bas Revel stockings to Cachou Lajaunie pastilles (tiny licorice candies used to sweeten breath after smoking). To capture the delight of a brand of French chocolate, he drew children romping with a giant chocolate bar. He drew a beautiful flapper holding "sunshine in a glass" to advertise the pleasures of drinking a brand of cognac (brandy).

A.M. Cassandre became famous for his ads that conveyed the speed, comfort, and grandeur of traveling by train and ocean liner. His stylized images—angular and exaggerated to give a sense of drama and movement—of the cruise ships S.S.

L'Atlantique, M.S. *Statendam* and S.S. *Normandie*, the latter a French ocean liner that entered service in 1936, immediately made many viewers want to take an ocean voyage.

American illustrator Joseph C. Leyendecker gained fame for his Arrow shirt ads, which made that company a household name in the 1920s. Leyendecker's ads featured the figure of a handsome, well-dressed young man who became known as the Arrow Collar Man. Arrow Collar ads were so compelling that the fictional character received fan mail, and President Theodore Roosevelt referred to the image as a superb portrait of the common man.

The "father of modern advertising," Leonetto Cappiello (1875–1942), was an Italian painter and poster designer.

Style-Setting Clothing

There were dozens of products to be advertised and sold, and style-setting clothing was at the top of the list. In the early

1920s, French designer Coco Chanel launched her revolutionary "garçonne look" (boyish look), which included short hair, dresses without waistlines, and daring women's trousers. A drastic change from earlier styles, the look was embraced by women who rushed to purchase it. Other designers followed with everything from formal apparel to sports and leisure wear. Those customers who could not afford designer clothing could purchase less expensive department store clothes or make their own using newly introduced paper patterns in the latest styles.

Accessories were "must-haves," too. Advertisements in *Good Housekeeping* and other magazines insisted that women buy shoes that were "smart" and "slender and suave in line."[36] Some shoes were virtual pieces of art deco. The Euclid shoe was, according to one ad, "whimsically adorned with diamonds, triangles, [and] lightning zigzags in vivid, effect contrast . . . for the fashionable Modernist gowns!"[37]

Few women had diamonds on their shoes, but many wore rhinestones on their wrists. Costume jewelry was art deco inspired and ranged from chunky Bakelite bracelets to long strings of glass beads and dress clips or pins with Egyptian motifs. Women also carried small beaded and fringed purses. These were covered with zigzag or some other art deco design and were useful for holding lipstick, powder compacts, and even small flasks of bootleg alcohol—all decorated in art deco design, too.

"Preoccupations of the Era"

Well-dressed men and women wanted to keep up appearances in their homes, and designers recognized that as another opportunity to showcase art deco designs. Private drinking parties were fashionable, and stylish equipment was necessary to make cocktails—mixed drinks that masked the taste of the cheap bathtub gin and moonshine whiskey that was produced during Prohibition.

Accessories needed to equip a home bar included ice buckets, cocktail shakers, soda dispensers, and glasses, just to name a few. Art deco–style barware was often made of chrome and glass, which created a smooth, shiny image while preventing

Auto manufacturers advertised to women in the 1920s, insisting that their lives would be better if they owned a car. Author Virginia Scharff explains their tactics in an excerpt from her book Taking the Wheel.

Ford Motor Company, in its first ever large-scale advertising campaign, promised readers of *The Ladies' Home Journal* that a Ford would be "An 'Open Door' to Wider Contacts," asserting that "By owning a Ford car a woman can with ease widen her sphere of interests without extra time or effort. She can accomplish more daily, yet easily keep pace with her usual schedule of domestic pursuits." Ford ads showed women in a variety of situations—vacationing, going shopping, visiting, and even conducting business, but always emphasized the social aspect of the product. No woman need feel lonesome, Ford implied, because "the car is so easy to drive that it constantly suggests thoughtful services to her friends. She can call for them without effort and share pleasantly their companionship."

Virginia Scharff, *Taking the Wheel: Women and the Coming of the Motor Age*. Albuquerque: University of New Mexico Press, 1992, pp. 141–42.

Her habit of measuring time in terms of dollars gives the woman in business keen insight into the true value of a Ford closed car for her personal use.

This car enables her to conserve minutes, to expedite her affairs, to widen the scope of her activities. Its low first cost, long life and inexpensive operation and upkeep convince her that it is a sound investment value.

And it is such a pleasant car to drive that it transforms the business call which might be an interruption into an enjoyable episode of her busy day.

TUDOR SEDAN, $590   FORDOR SEDAN, $685   COUPE, $525   (All prices f. o. b. Detroit)

Ford
CLOSED CARS

May 1924 Good Housekeeping

This 1924 Ford Motor Company ad from Good Housekeeping *magazine was aimed directly at women.*

rust. Sleek and futuristic-looking globes and airships were popular shaker shapes. So were clear or colored glass shakers in barbell shapes and shakers in shapes of animals, ships' lanterns, and bells.

Cocktail glasses were often "naughty," with stems designed in the shape of nude women supporting the cup itself. Gaston writes, "The 'global' liqueur set, the 'Zeppelin' bar, and the 'dancing nude' cocktail stem definitely define several of the preoccupations of the era—world communication, speed, relaxed morals, and most of all, fun!"[38]

Smoking in Style

Women and men smoked as well as drank, so tobacco-related products were also popular. Pocket lighters were a must for those on the go, and silver- or gold-plated lighters engraved with art deco sunbursts or geometric lines made a modern statement. There were also art deco–style lighters with tortoise shell accents, with leather coverings, and with gold plate and mother-of-pearl geometric designs.

In homes, tabletop lighters expressed art deco in their endless elaborate shapes. Some looked like animals, others like sphinxes. Some included clocks or held matches. A few even introduced more up-to-date mechanisms, an art deco theme. For instance, in 1926 Ronson invented the "automatic operation" Banjo lighter that could be worked with one hand. Ronson's Touch Tip lighters featured a wand whose tip could be ignited when the lighter produced a spark, eliminating the need for matches.

With many people smoking, ashtrays were necessities and came in a multitude of styles. Some were tabletop; some stood on the floor. The most daring incorporated an art deco–styled nude female figure. There were also "silent butlers"—long handled, lidded containers in which overflowing ashtrays could be dumped. They were usually art deco designs in shiny chrome or aluminum with Bakelite or wooden handles.

The Art Deco Room

Couples who were well-to-do often hired interior designers to give their homes a complete art deco look. Most people, however, were lucky if they could afford even one large piece that could be a focal point of their living room or dining room.

There were many exciting things from which to choose. Ruhlmann designed understated but elegant chairs, daybeds, and cabinets in rare, exotic woods. German American Ludwig Mies Van der Rohe's unique pieces included Barcelona chairs made of bent steel and leather straps, and cantilevered chairs with no back legs, made of steel tubes and leather lacing. Hungarian-born Marcel Breuer made simple tubular steel and aluminum pieces.

Other designers offered more conspicuous elegance. Swiss designer Jean Dunand used enameling over metal to create dramatic screens with geometric and Asian designs. French artists Louis Sue and Andre Mare combined gold, marble, and

The Farnsworth House in Illinois, is one of the few residential buildings in America created by Mies Van der Rohe. His architectural designs were as unique as his furniture.

marquetry for ornate looks. Marquetry is a technique in which decorative patterns of bone, ivory, or some other material are inset onto a piece of furniture. French interior designer Jean-Michel Frank's furniture was simple in shape but covered with luxurious shagreen or straw marquetry, in which he split and processed pieces of wheat or oat straw. He then painstakingly applied the straw to furniture surfaces to create rich geometric patterns in tones that ranged from pale gold to deep brown.

Electric Deco

While not everyone could afford high deco, most families could afford a less expensive art deco piece. In many cases this was a radio. There were no televisions at the time, so radios were often centers of the home where families gathered in the evening to listen to music or special entertainment programs. As the center of the home, style was important. Some radios were encased in wooden cabinets decorated with metalwork in geometric and floral patterns. Portable models were encased in Bakelite or Catalin plastic cases in streamlined rectangular designs.

Electricity came into many homes in the 1920s, which meant that kerosene and gas lamps were replaced by electric table and floor lamps. While plain lamps were everywhere, art deco lamps were popular and came in many designs. Some

Neon lights illuminate the night along Ocean Beach Drive in Miami, Florida's art deco district.

incorporated female figures. Others used fan shapes, lightning bolts, and other geometric designs. Torchère lamps—pole lamps topped with flared glass shades that reflect light upward—were popular, too. Some of these, like French designer Edgar Brandt's bronze serpent lamp, were works of art. Brandt used an elongated snake for the body, with the head coiled to hold the glass shade. There were also art deco chandeliers, and in upscale new homes, interior designers experimented with indirect lighting. Lights were placed strategically in the ceiling or on the wall to create a mood or highlight a feature of a room.

Neon lighting was rarely found in homes in the 1920s; it was more common in public places. The first neon lights were seen in the United States in 1923, when a car dealer in Los Angeles began using them as an advertising scheme on his lot. The lights were visible even in daylight and attracted fascinated passersby, who nicknamed them "liquid fire." By the 1930s neon lights were an important part of art deco design, particularly on elaborate theater marquees (entrances). Scrolls, zigzags, stars, and other multicolored neon shapes drew patrons to the so-called picture palaces. New York journalist Christopher Gray recalled the humming noise the neon lighting made: "The lights buzzing on the underside of the marquee, when they were on, enveloped the passerby in a warm, glowing field."[39]

Style-Setting Clocks

Clocks were just as important as lamps in homes of the 1920s and 1930s. Style-setting families often purchased art deco clocks, which were popular conversation pieces and came in an endless number of designs. Some were simple, such as the "golden hour" electric clock by Jefferson Electric with a brass base and rim and a face of transparent glass. Some were multifunctional, such as those made of marble with matching side vases for flowers. Many were elaborate, made of brass and onyx or decorated with birds or leaping deer.

French art deco clocks were expensive and purchased only by the well-to-do. Artist Jean Goulden's highly geometric clocks, for instance, were made of metals such as silver and

GIANT OF INDUSTRIAL DESIGN

One of the most prolific art deco designers was Walter Dorwin Teague, born in Indiana in 1883. Inspired by the work of Le Corbusier, a pioneer of modern architecture and design, he became an industrial designer and in 1927 began work for the Eastman Kodak Camera company, the first of many design projects he carried out for high-profile companies over time.

Under contract to Kodak, Teague first created the Vanity Kodak Ensemble, a color-coordinated camera, lipstick holder, compact, mirror, and change purse, targeted to appeal to young flappers. He also designed the Beau Brownie, an instant camera in a Bakelite box with art deco geometric enameled patterns on the front. "They're gay. And colorful. With just enough of the modern touch to give them Parisian smartness,"[1] a Kodak advertisement claimed.

In 1937 the Texaco oil company commissioned Teague to design a modern gas station for them. In what would become a model for generations of stations, Teague created an office area with large plate-glass windows for display of tires, a service center, and a covered area over the gas pumps. The company logo was prominently displayed on the upper facade of the station.

In 1946 Teague began designing for the aerospace and defense giant Boeing Company. His association with Boeing continued for the rest of his life, with his studio working on every Boeing aircraft that was built during that time. Teague died in 1960 at the age of ninety-four, but his company, Teague, continues the work he started in the art deco era.

1. The Kodak Girl Collection, "Here's a Christmas Favorite in a New Paris Garb," advertisement, 1930s. www.kodakgirl.com/kgmisc16.htm.

The Vanity Kodak Ensemble camera created by Walter Dorwin Teague was a camera with matching compact, lipstick holder, mirror, and change purse.

bronze and covered with enamel work. Enamel is a substance, often melted glass, that is applied to the surface of metal or glass to make a hard, shiny decorative surface. Goulden was known for his champlevé method of enameling. Champlevé ("raised field") was a process in which troughs or cells were carved into the surface of a metal object, then filled with powdered colored glass. The piece was fired (baked) in a kiln (furnace or oven) until the enamel melted. When completed, the unenameled portions of the metal surface remained visible as a frame for the enamel designs.

In contrast to elaborate French clocks, inexpensive timepieces with art deco lines were manufactured by companies such as Smiths English Clocks of England. Smiths was also one of the first companies to produce synchronous electric clocks, whose motor stayed in step with reversals of the alternating electric current that was common at the time. The Smiths Sectric models came in wall or mantle versions and were made of Bakelite or some other type of plastic. All were sleek, simple, and affordable.

In the Kitchen

Purchasing a radio, a decorative electric lamp, and a clock or two was only the beginning for most 1920s homemakers. Even working women spent a great deal of time in the kitchen, and advertisements alerted them to the fact that new products were available to make their lives more enjoyable. Those products ranged from streamlined Electrolux vacuum cleaners to sunburst candle holders, animal-shaped salt and pepper shakers, and, of course, colorful dishes for the table.

For those who could afford it, British potter Clarice Cliff's Bizarre Ware line of hand-painted tableware was extremely popular. However, designer Frederick Hurten Rhead's American-made Fiestaware was more affordable. Fiestaware featured simple, rugged plates, bowls, and cups in solid, bold colors. The line was marketed by playing on the image of a Mexican fiesta, and an early advertisement hailed it as "the dinnerware that turns your table into a celebration."[40]

With the coming of the Great Depression, few could spare money for fine dinnerware, and new types of dishes that became known as Depression glass took their place. Depression glass was clear or colored, translucent glass. Light could pass through it, but not with clarity. It could be purchased in five-and-dime stores such as Woolworth's and Ben Franklin's and was sometimes distributed free in boxes of cereal or laundry soap as an incentive to buy the product. Although less well made and of lower quality glass than earlier art deco glass, much of it had the geometric patterns that were common to the style.

Glassware Decor

Art deco glassware was another affordable way to add new decorative touches to a home. In addition to kitchenware, there were glass flower vases in a variety of colors and designs, ceramic trays and decorative bowls, and glass figures in the shape of people and animals to set on shelves or small tables.

Art deco glass designers were not content just to create unusual shapes; they came up with new or almost-forgotten techniques to make different colors and textures of glass, too. For instance, they etched glass by covering parts of their design, then bathing the rest in acid, which dissolved away portions and created patterns. They made opalescent glass pieces by adding phosphates and other minerals to molten glass before it was molded. The result was a milky, rainbow color characteristic of an opal. For those with money to spend, the French foundries of Marius-Ernest Sabino and Edmond Etling et Cie produced many beautiful opalescent pieces of glassware in the 1920s and 1930s. Maurice Marinot and the Daum glassworks factory made beautiful etched pieces in France as well.

Marinot and another French artist, Marcel Goupy, were also known for the enameling they put on their glass designs. They first mixed pigment colors into ground glass, then painted it onto a piece and fired it in a kiln. Goupy was known for his pieces that featured images such as nudes, jazz musicians, stylized flowers, and birds.

Premier Glassmaker

René Lalique was one of the premier glassmakers of the period, renowned for his glass vases and figurines as well as his stunning perfume bottles and glass jewelry. Unlike other craftspeople, Lalique worked with demicrystal, which had only half the lead content needed for glass to be labeled "crystal" under French law. Critics did not believe that well-made pieces could be made of demicrystal, but Lalique proved them wrong and inspired other decorators to use the material as well.

In addition to working with demicrystal, Lalique created pieces using *pâté de verre* or glass paste. He mixed finely crushed glass particles with metallic oxides and a binding agent and packed the paste into a desired mold. He then fired the piece in a kiln. The resulting glass was a swirl of colors with a

A selection of perfume bottles in various designs by René Lalique.

translucent look and a slightly waxy feel. By varying the components and the time in the kiln, Lalique came up with different textures and colors to produce different looks.

Lalique's perfume bottles created a greater sensation than his *pâté de verre* work, however. In early times even expensive perfumes were packaged in plain flasks. Around 1907, however, Lalique formed a partnership with French perfume manufacturer François Coty. Coty created fragrances, and Lalique created designer bottles for them. The bottles varied from simple tubular green glass with beehive-shaped stoppers to etched bottles with delicate fan-shaped or figural stoppers. Each was considered a work of art. Lalique created more than 250 different styles of perfume bottles for Coty as well as bottles for perfume manufacturers Worth, Forvil, Houbigant, and others.

ART DECO SILVER

Architect and designer William Spratling had no idea he would spend his life designing Mayan revival deco jewelry when he discovered the mountain village of Taxco in Mexico the 1930s. Taxco had once been a silver-mining town, but the mines had been closed. Inspired by the region, Spratling hired a goldsmith to come to Taxco to make silver pieces he had sketched. His designs used Native American and traditional motifs such as circular discs, straps, and ropes and incorporated gold, copper, brass, and occasionally abalone shell into the work.

Spratling's jewelry quickly became popular, motivating him to expand his operation. He also began an apprenticeship program for others interested in designing in silver. More artists joined the movement, and by 1941 Spratling's silver jewelry was being sold to well-to-do customers in high-end department stores such as Neiman Marcus and Saks Fifth Avenue in New York City.

Lalique's stunning vases and delicate perfume bottles were priceless contributions to art deco design, and they stood in stark contrast to the steel, cement, and granite pieces created by art deco architects and industrial designers during the 1920s and 1930s. Cars, trains, ships, and buildings were all designed to have art deco looks during those decades, and it was in the more public pieces that the style exhibited all the jazzy, geometric, streamlined details that won it so many fans and followers.

Architectural Modernism

Art deco furnishings added elegant and whimsical touches to living rooms, dining rooms, and kitchens around the world, but the style was more visible outside the home. From steamships to skyscrapers, designers expressed their vision of modernistic style using steel, stone, and stucco. Historian of architecture John Tauranac observes, "Art deco . . . began as a movement in furniture and decorative arts, but its influence in one form or other extended beyond interiors and magazine covers . . . to the design of automobiles and even locomotives."[41]

Motoring in Style

In the 1920s "motorcars," as automobiles were called at the time, were boxy and built high off the ground. They became increasingly long, low, and aerodynamic-looking, however, as designers incorporated streamline moderne style into their designs. Hoods were elongated. Multiple horizontal lines of chrome were added on the sides to give a feeling of movement. Bodies and roofs were lowered. Windshields were tipped back. Fenders swooped down into running boards (small ledges beneath the doors to assist passengers entering or leaving), and the rear of the car sloped down to a point. By the end of the 1930s, cars were almost unrecognizable as the same machines that had preceded them in the 1920s.

Cars were designed to look more luxurious, too, with better upholstery and more chrome. The hood ornament or car mascot added to the luxury. In the 1920s and 1930s, radiator caps were set on the top of the hood, and car designers realized that these figural ornaments could be attached to the caps

The need for radiator caps on cars in the 1920s inspired many carmakers to produce innovative art deco hood ornaments to go over the caps.

to advertise the car's make. Art deco themes of speed and movement came to mind whenever car design was concerned, so most ornaments were not only art deco in stylization, they expressed those themes in some way. For instance, Packard radiators were topped with Nike, the goddess of speed, with her hair streaming back into the air. Jaguar used a springing jaguar. Franklin Airman cars had a small airplane with a spinning propeller. The ornaments were chrome-plated metal so as to be shiny and noticeable. Companies such as Pontiac and DeSoto went so far as to build a lightbulb into their designs to light up the figures at night.

Soon independent designers recognized the market for hood ornaments. They began creating their own art deco pieces that could be purchased and installed on radiator caps. The ornaments were made of metal or glass and came in a variety of colors. Lalique was the most famous to create such ornaments. He originally produced twenty-seven different styles in the shape of animals, birds, and insects like butterflies and dragonflies. Lalique's most famous and largest ornament was Victoire or Spirit of the Wind, an exquisite woman's head with hair streaming behind. The 10-inch-long piece (25.4cm) was displayed in the 1928 Paris Motor Show, mounted on the hood of a Minerva, a world-famous brand of race car owned by movie stars and royalty. In 1931 Lalique also designed a special running greyhound ornament for Prince George of England.

When Zephyrus Blows

While affecting auto styles, art deco also influenced train design. In the 1920s passenger rail travel in America was at an all-time high, with over 1 million passengers riding more than 47 million miles (75.64 million km) on trains every day. When the Great Depression struck, however, railroads began to lose money as passengers cut back on travel. Faced with disaster, Ralph Budd, president of Burlington Railway, decided to do something to revive business. His idea was to lure passengers back with an up-to-date train system that was not only comfortable but speedy, too.

In 1931 Budd met with several talented designers to devise a plan for a new train. Former automobile manufacturer Edward G. Budd (no relation) was enlisted because he had come up with a method of making stainless steel into shapes while preserving its strength and rust resistance. Stainless steel was lighter than the iron used in traditional locomotives and would allow the train to move faster. Aeronautical engineer Albert Gardner Dean was hired to design a shape for the train. He used the streamline moderne style to create a sloping nose that reduced air resistance. He also lowered the train's center of gravity to keep it from tipping as it sped around corners. Architect John Harbeson and industrial designer Paul Philippe Cret created horizontal grooves down the sides, which added to the streamlined effect. In addition to having an elegant exterior design, the interior of the train featured luxuries like air-conditioning, indirect lighting, and cushioned seats to make the passengers more comfortable.

Burlington Railway's *Zephyr* train had a streamlined moderne style that reduced air resistance. The train also featured luxuries like air-conditioning and cushioned seats.

For advertising purposes, the new streamlined train needed a catchy name. Budd had been reading Geoffrey Chaucer's book *The Canterbury Tales* during the design process. In the book, Zephyrus, the gentle and nurturing west wind, motivated pilgrims to set off on a journey. Budd decided to name his new train the *Zephyr*.

Streamliners

Before the *Zephyr* could be introduced, the Union Pacific Railroad introduced its own streamlined train, the *M-10,000*, which it soon renamed the *City of Salina*. Famed engineer Martin P. Blomberg helped design the exterior, which featured a slanted duralumin (aluminum alloy) body and a nose shaped in parabolic (half circle) arches. Because bright art deco colors were popular, the train was painted bright yellow with a brown roof and undersides. A line of red separated the colors. The interior featured more subdued art deco style that included indirect lighting, pale colors, and unusual cork tile on floors.

Beginning in February 1934, crowds gathered along tracks to the watch the *M-10,000*. The train's fame was soon eclipsed by Burlington's *Zephyr*, however. On May 26, 1934, the *Zephyr* made a widely advertized "Dawn to Dusk" run from Denver to Chicago. On the trip it averaged 77.6 miles per hour (124.8kmh) and hit a top speed of 104 miles per hour (167.4kmh), earning it world speed records and legions of fans.

The *Zephyr* was such a star that streamlined trains became all the rage. Other Zephyr streamliners were built and put into service by Burlington. The Chicago, Milwaukee, St. Paul and Pacific Railroad also introduced a line of streamlined diesel trains called Hiawathas. In 1934 the Atchison, Topeka & Santa Fe Railroad's streamliner, the *Super Chief*, began running between Chicago and Los Angeles twice a week. The Seaboard Railway inaugurated the *Silver Meteor* between New York and Miami on February 2, 1939. For a time in the late 1930s, the ten fastest trains in the world were all American streamliners.

The Golden Age of Ocean Liners

Streamliners were useful to travel across America, but travelers going overseas between 1900 and World War II usually went by ship. Passenger air travel had not yet developed. The busiest sea route was across the North Atlantic Ocean, and a great many historic ocean liners, including the *Lusitania*, *Mauretania*, *Britannic*, and *Bismarck*, carried passengers between Europe and North America early in the century. Journalist Anindita Dasgupta explains, "During the 'golden age' of ocean liners (between the end of the 19th century and World War II), passenger lines competed to produce not only the most comfortable, but also the fastest and safest ships."[42]

Several new ships built during this period featured art deco style. The first was the SS *Ile de France*, which set out on its maiden voyage on June 22, 1927, from Le Havre, France. Heralded as the "Queen of the Sea," its interior was elegant

One of SS *Normandie*'s spacious dining salons is shown as a background in an exhibit of the ship's art deco–inspired dining tables and chairs.

but emphasized simple geometric lines in contrast to the dark, heavily ornate interiors of earlier liners.

The ship was a delight to art deco lovers. In the lacquer-and-gold Grand Salon, forty sleek columns rose around the walls, surrounding a 1,000-square-foot dance floor (93 sq. m). The three-story dining room was decorated in three shades of gray marble with stripes of gold. Guests entered by a wrought-iron staircase and, according to a 1927 article in *Literary Digest*, were treated to the sight of a fountain "of round gold and silver pipes, with a center silver light."[43] Throughout the ship an indirect lighting system gave passengers the impression of being in warm sunshine. Each first-class cabin had its own unique decor. A garage on board held sixty cars. A shooting gallery, gymnasium, French shops, and a merry-go-round added to the amenities.

The *Normandie*

The *Ile de France* lost some of its sparkle when France's SS *Normandie* entered service in 1935. The *Normandie* was the largest ship built up to that time and combined the best and the latest of features both inside and out. Russian naval engineer Vladimir Yourkevitch designed a new shape for the front of the vessel—a slanting bow that widened dramatically beneath the waterline. The shape changed the way water flowed around the ship, allowing it to move faster. As a result, it could cross the Atlantic in recording-breaking time.

Inside, the *Normandie*'s public rooms were spacious and filled with pieces designed specifically for it by the finest French art deco designers, coordinated by architect Roger-Henri Expert. The main dining room had 20-foot doors (6.1m) that were decorated with bronze medallions created by French decorator Raymond Subes. The room was lighted indirectly by twelve tall glass pillars designed by Lalique. Lalique also designed chandeliers that earned the ship the nickname "Ship of Light." The Grand Salon was paneled in lacquer-and-glass murals designed by Jean Dupas. First-class passenger suites featured dining rooms, baby grand pianos, multiple bedrooms, and private decks. "It was the gem upon the sea," says maritime historian William Miller. "It was a Goddess. . . . It had a spacious quality. It oozed art deco. It even smelled of expensive French perfume from bow to stern. It was . . . a palace on water."[44]

Despite its glory, the *Normandie* came to a sad end during World War II. Seized by U.S. authorities to be used for the war effort, it was taken to New York and converted to a troopship. In 1942, while being loaded with supplies, a fire broke out on board. The fire spread and, to everyone's horror, the ship capsized. Fortunately, most of the art and decorative items had already been removed. Other pieces were rescued when the ship was salvaged and cut up for scrap in 1946.

Architectural Achievements

Trains and ships offered fine opportunities for streamline moderne design to be displayed, but homes and public buildings were canvasses for a wider range of art deco style. From Europe and Asia to South America and Africa, they were built in classic moderne, zigzag moderne, and streamline moderne styles as well as regional variations that set them apart.

In Havana, Cuba, designers created art deco government buildings, sports arenas, and private homes using native wood, ornamental grillwork, and Caribbean motifs such as tropical fruits and birds. In the city of Durban, South Africa, designers decorated buildings with raised designs that recalled the city's maritime and Muslim history. In the city of Asmara in the tiny country of Eritrea in Africa, art deco had an Italian influence. The country was developed in the 1930s by Italian colonizers who decided to look to the future when they designed the city. Today the most unusual building in the town is the Fiat Tagliero gas station, designed by Guiseppe Pettazzi. It resembles a streamlined airplane with 96-foot-long concrete wings (29.3m).

Although art deco architecture sprang up throughout the world, it flourished in the United States. With an abundance of talented designers and many open spaces on which to build, commercial buildings and private homes became examples of

San Francisco's famous Golden Gate Bridge is an art deco masterpiece that owes its style to Irving F. Morrow and his wife Gertrude C. Morrow. While the suspension design of the bridge itself was a result of input from many architects and designers, the Morrows determined that its light posts would have clean, angled forms. They added wide, vertical ribbing to the horizontal tower braces to accent the sun's light on the structure. They simplified the heavy pedestrian railings to be uniform posts, wide enough apart so motorists would have unobstructed views.

The Morrow's most visible contribution to the bridge, however, was the bright red orange paint that was chosen to cover it. Others had suggested that the span be painted aluminum or dull gray and argued that no red paint would stand up to the damp, salty air of the Bay Area. Morrow convinced them otherwise, however, and the bridge stands today, a symbol of art deco elegance, refinement, and sophistication.

San Francisco's art deco masterpiece, the Golden Gate Bridge, was designed by husband and wife team Irving and Gertrude Morrow.

the many faces of the style. "They stood as the architectural capstone [crowning achievement] for the twenties in America, and they still fill us with a sense of awe,"[45] writes Tauranac of the many buildings that were built.

Lily Pads and Champagne Bottles

One extraordinary example of an art deco commercial building is the Johnson Wax Company administration building in Racine, Wisconsin. It was created by Frank Lloyd Wright in 1936. Wright designed the building in streamlined style with curved walls both inside and out. Steel-reinforced columns extend from floor to ceiling and look like stylized lily pads holding up the roof. Glass tubing lets in light, eliminating the need for windows and providing a soft, shadowless look.

The company's nearby fourteen-story Research Tower is shaped like a stylized tree. Its interior levels alternate between round and square floors, which creates what Wright called an "open corners" plan. This originally allowed for easy communication between floors and gave workers a sense of space. Wright wrote, "There in the Johnson Building you catch no sense of enclosure whatever at any angle, top or sides. . . . Interior space comes free, you are not aware of any boxing in at all. . . . Right there where you've always experienced this interior constriction you take a look at the sky!"[46]

Two more unique examples of art deco public buildings are the Carbide and Carbon Building on Michigan Avenue in Chicago and the American Standard (Radiator) Building in New York City. The former was designed by American architects Daniel Burnham and Hubert Burnham to resemble a dark green champagne bottle with gold foil. The building's base is covered in polished black granite, and its tower is dark green terra-cotta with gold leaf accents. The Radiator Building was created with pinnacles and terra-cotta bands that are covered with gold, and the base is bronze and black granite, covered with carved figures symbolizing the transformation of matter into energy.

Chicago's Carbide and Carbon Building's art deco-inspired design was meant to resemble a champagne bottle with gold foil.

Skyscrapers

It was with skyscrapers, however, that designers in the United States took art deco to new levels. Faced with limited land to build on and city zoning laws that decreed that buildings had to be smaller on top than at the base, they designed them upward and inward. Fortunately, the development of steel "skeleton frames," faster elevators, and more powerful water pumps for plumbing allowed them to create the designs they conceived.

The result of all their designing was a new style—a pencil- or pyramid-shaped building that pointed dramatically skyward. With their height and pointed domes, the 1,454-foot Empire State Building (443m) and the 1,046-foot Chrysler Building (319m) were only the first of many examples of the unique new building shape that was soon seen in other cities. Author Eric P. Nash and photographer Norman McGrath observe, "By the end of the 1920s the setback skyscraper, originally built in response to a New York zoning code, became a style that caught on from Chicago to Shanghai."[47]

The Chrysler Building and the Empire State Building were the two tallest art deco skyscrapers built in the 1920s and 1930s. The most ambitious skyscraper project in the United States, however, was Rockefeller Center, the largest private construction plan ever undertaken up to that time. Construction began in May 1930 and was completed in November 1939. Built by the Rockefeller family and guided by renowned American architect Raymond Hood, three architectural firms cooperated to design and construct fourteen buildings of streamline moderne design on 22 acres (8.9ha) of ground in downtown Manhattan. Dozens of art deco pieces—murals, raised figures, and statues—throughout the center make it an art deco showpiece both in its architecture and its decor. Architectural critic Lewis Mumford declared after it was complete that it was "architecturally the most exciting mass of buildings in the city."[48]

Rockefeller Center

One of the centerpieces of Rockefeller Center is the GE Building (not to be confused with the General Electric Building, also in New York City). Because it was built during the Great Depression when there was no money for decorative spires and figures high in the air, it is more streamlined than ornate. Instead, its designers created its granite and limestone exterior to look dramatically different when viewed from different angles. From Fifth Avenue it appears to be a narrow shaft. From Sixth Avenue it is an enormous rectangle, which earned it its nicknames "The Rock" and "The Slab."

What art deco ornamentation there is on the building was placed at street level, where it could be best seen and appreciated. American sculptor Lee Lawrie created an elaborate painted and gold-covered sculpture above the main entrance that depicts the figure *Wisdom* shoving away the clouds of ignorance. Similar sculptures of *Sound* and *Light* were placed

Radio City Music Hall's designers chose an art deco design that incorporated glass, aluminum, chrome, and geometric ornamentation to create a stunning effect.

to the right and left. In front of the building, American sculptor Paul Manship created a bronze gilded statue of the Greek character Prometheus bringing fire to mankind.

Another art deco gem of Rockefeller Center is Radio City Music Hall, housed in the RKO Building. The building itself was designed to be a simple, vertically striped limestone facade with pyramidal shapes on one side. The theater's marquee, like so many other deco theaters built during the period, was streamlined with curves and neon lighting. Inside the six-thousand-seat music hall, however, American designers Edward Durell Stone and Donald Deskey incorporated glass, aluminum, chrome, and geometric ornamentation to create a stunning art deco effect. Weber writes, "This magnificent combination movie-vaudeville theater conjured up a spectacular dream world of zigzag-style pattern, imagery and lighting effects."[49]

Deco Homes

In addition to skyscrapers, private homes could be art deco gems, too. The Lovell House in Los Angeles, designed by Richard Neutra in 1927 for physician Philip Lovell, was the first steel-frame house in the United States. Built on the side of a hill, it is geometric in shape, with balconies suspended by cables from the roof and a pool hung in a U-shaped concrete cradle. Its rooms have high ceilings and are simple and airy. Wide expanses of windows allow for stunning views of the surrounding landscape.

The Butler House of Des Moines, Iowa, designed by George Kraetsch and Earl Butler, was described as the most modern house in the world when it was built in 1934. Streamlined on its exterior, its interior is divided into two halves, which are separated by a central ramp that runs from the basement to the top of the house. Floors lead off the ramp on seven half levels. Thus, the floors on the western half of the house are 4 feet 9 inches (1.45m) lower than those on the eastern half. When it was built, the house was equipped with a sophisticated telephone system, a freezer that could make over six hundred ice cubes at a time, and a dining room ceiling of colored lights operated by dimmer switches so that any desired color or intensity could be obtained.

Dramatic art deco homes were built in other countries, too. One of the most unusual private residences in England, called High and Over, was designed by New Zealand architect Amyas Connell. Built in 1929, the house is in the shape of a Y, with three arms projecting out of a central hall. The roof is flat; the walls are cement-covered brick. Flat concrete canopies supported by columns project out of the roof like airplane wings. The original interior was as unusual as the exterior. Some walls were painted orange. Others were jade green accented with chrome. The hall was paved with black marble, and a fountain in the center shot a stream of water as high as the first-floor gallery. Interior doors were made of steel and glass. Lights were concealed behind glass panels. The style was not appreciated by traditional British architects at the time, but as Tinniswood notes, "More than seventy years after it was finished, its hard, white angles and blind, staring windows startle the eye. . . . It is architecture at its most provocative."[50]

Los Angeles Deco

In the United States, fast-growing regions like Los Angeles often ended up with large blocks of modern homes in art deco style. Much building in the 1920s and 1930s took place in residential districts such as Hancock Park, Beverly Hills, West Hollywood, and Hollywood Hills. Cowboy actor Tom Mix and comedian Buster Keaton were just two famous residents who lived in elaborate art deco villas that were built in those neighborhoods.

Los Angeles produced as many public deco buildings as private ones. Los Angeles City Hall is an art deco skyscraper with decorative friezes and geometric lines. The art deco James Oviatt office building includes decorative glass elements designed by Lalique. The Eastern Columbia Building, headquarters of the Eastern Outfitting Company and the Columbia Outfitting Company, was designed by American architect Claud Beelman and built in 1930. It is covered with glossy turquoise terra-cotta trimmed with deep blue and gold. The

DARING AND EXPERIMENTAL

Frank Lloyd Wright was one of America's most influential twentieth-century architects and designers. He was instrumental in creating the American tradition of modern decoration upon which American art deco was built.

Born in Wisconsin on June 8, 1867, Wright completed fifty of his own projects by the age of thirty-four. Many of them were "Prairie Houses," so called because the design complemented America's mid-western landscape. Most were low buildings with shallow, sloping roofs, clean lines, open spaces, overhangs, and terraces. All were modern and angular, with a sleek look that was later seen in streamline moderne. Wright's Mayan revival style homes of the 1920s were more typical of art deco, with pyramid shapes and elaborate ornamentation.

Throughout his life, Wright promoted "organic architecture"—a style that emphasizes harmony between buildings and nature. He was a prolific worker, designing more than a thousand projects, which resulted in more than five hundred completed works. In 1937, however, he began work on one of his dreams—a planned community called "Usonia" in Pleasantville, New York. The community was laid out in a circular manner, following the natural flow of the land. The homes fit into the land, too. They were small, single story, and L-shaped with flat roofs and large overhangs for passive solar heating and natural cooling. Forty-seven homes were built there, and the community continues to the present.

Wright died in 1959, but many of his buildings remain. They are reminders of a forward-thinking artist who personified the daring, experimental spirit of the art deco period.

Even Wright's early, more traditional designs like the Nathan G. Moore House in Oak Park, Illinois, exhibit Mayan ornamentation and cantilevered porches.

building's face is decorated with sunburst patterns, geometric shapes, zigzags, and stylized animal and plant forms. Even surrounding sidewalks are art deco, made of multicolored tile patterned with zigzags and other shapes.

Art deco buildings were built along the Miracle Mile, an upscale shopping district on Wilshire Boulevard in Los Angeles that was established in the early 1920s by developer A.W. Ross. Ross dreamed of creating a business district that exuded prosperity and luxury. He approved builders that used only the most up-to-date construction methods and added elaborate art deco details to their buildings that made each look like a work of art. For instance, the Beverly/Poinsettia commercial building (set diagonally on the corner of Beverly Boulevard and Poinsettia Place) was created with columns, a pyramid-shaped tower, and a Vitrolite sunburst above the entrance. The upscale decor did indeed help fulfill Ross's dream because it attracted better businesses and more shoppers to the district.

The Los Angeles City Hall art deco skyscraper is known for its decorative friezes and geometric lines.

During the Great Depression, many artists worked at government-sponsored projects so they could make a living and help the country at the same time. In Oklahoma, where unemployment reached record levels, thousands of men found work under the directorship of the government's Works Progress Administration (WPA).

In the capital of Tulsa, architects and designers created dozens of beautiful public buildings, including schools, fairground pavilions, and fire stations. From the Tulsa Union Depot, built in 1931, to Will Rogers High School, built in 1939, the lines of the buildings, the brickwork, and the ornamental detail were superbly art deco. On the latter building, for instance, tall brick columns are topped with terra-cotta friezes. Ornamentation is everywhere, but the focus is on panels above the double front doors. These feature cowboy-turned-actor Will Rogers's life in two phases. One depicts his cowboy days with a horse, roped steer, and the prairie, the other his movie days with a reel, a camera, and the airplane in which he met his death in August 1935.

Hollywood Deco

In Los Angeles, Hollywood moviemakers and stars did as much to further art deco style as any architect or interior designer. Between 60 million and 90 million Americans went to the movies each week in the 1930s, drawn into newly built theaters whose interiors were decorated with the most luxurious art deco designs—tropical images, filigree ceilings, scrolled pillars, and elaborate lighting. Audiences watched and identified with stars such as Greta Garbo, Joan Crawford, Fred Astaire, and Ginger Rogers, whose on-screen lives were spent in art deco homes, on luxurious art deco–designed ships, and in exotic art deco–inspired nightclubs. After seeing them, even the most ordinary housewives left the theater determined to add elegance to their lives with a new bedroom suite or a set of art deco barware. Author Susan A. Sternau writes, "Promoted in Hollywood as the style of the stars, art deco made the transition in a few short years from a primarily French style to a universally understood symbol of glamour."[51]

Cedric Gibbons was responsible for the art deco look of dozens of Hollywood movies. He was head of the Metro Goldwyn Mayer (MGM) Studio's art department, which gave him a chance to oversee all the sets and props that were made at the time. In addition, he had a taste for streamline moderne. MGM historian Gary Carey writes, "All [Gibbons's] designs were drawn in accordance with what he called his philosophy of the uncluttered—they were clean, functional and often highly stylized, a look that was to cause a major revolution in movie décor."[52]

While Gibbons influenced audiences with his set design, Busby Berkeley choreographed art deco into his films. Berkeley movies regularly featured musical numbers in which dozens of women, dressed alike, moved in synchrony to make shifting kaleidoscope-like patterns. For instance, in one scene from *Footlight Parade*, swimmers float on their backs, form rotating circles, and move their arms and legs to create zigzag designs. Later they pose on a tiered rotating pedestal to recreate a stylized fountain pattern.

The public's enthusiasm for Hollywood and the movies was limitless, but their enthusiasm for art deco waned in the 1940s. They stopped buying the style and began neglecting the many architectural gems of the period, allowing them to fall into decay. Author Susannah Harris Stone writes, "An obstacle to . . . restoration . . . was the fact that art deco had not yet been given the full measure of appreciation it later received as an architectural style."[53] That appreciation had to wait for new generations who could see the playful, quirky style from a new perspective. Only then would it get the recognition and respect that it lacked during its heyday.

Deco Revival

A rt deco lost popularity after the 1930s primarily because of the start of World War II. Fighting began in Europe in 1939. The United States entered the conflict after Pearl Harbor, Hawaii, was bombed by the Japanese navy in 1941. After that, no one cared about impressing their friends with playful ashtrays or skyscraper-shaped chairs. "Reuse" and "make do" were rallying cries as everyone sacrificed to provide money and equipment for the troops. Author Stanley K. Schultz observes, "The necessities of war even influenced American fashion. In the spring of 1942, the War Production Board became the nation's premier clothing consultant by dictating styles for civilian apparel that would conserve cloth and metal for the war effort."[54]

The conservative style that followed art deco became known as midcentury modern design. Rather than luxurious and playful, it was modest and sober. Even more so than streamline moderne, which could be elegant and include details such as curved lines and round windows, midcentury modern was extremely simple, straight, and practical.

Homes were small, designed and furnished to just meet the needs of the average family. Single-story ranch homes

Located in West Hollywood, the Sunset Tower Hotel was designed in 1929 by architect Leland A. Bryant and is considered one of the finest examples of art deco architecture in the Los Angeles area. Plaster bands decorated with plants, animals, mythological creatures, and dirigibles march around its sides, while a stylized pineapple sits atop its tower. Even the entrance of the parking garage in the rear is decorated with a sculptured panel of a 1920s automobile.

Many Hollywood celebrities called the Sunset Tower home in the 1930s. They included Marilyn Monroe, Clark Gable, Frank Sinatra, and even gangster Bugsy Siegel. Billionaire Howard Hughes kept a number of suites for his various girlfriends. John Wayne lived in the penthouse

for a time and allegedly kept a cow on the balcony so that fresh milk was always available.

The building went through a period of decline in the early 1980s and barely escaped being demolished. It was saved and renovated, however, and has been operated as a luxury hotel under the names The Argyle, the St. James Club, and most recently the Sunset Tower Hotel. It was added to the National Register of Historic Places in 1980.

The Sunset Tower Hotel, with a long history of being home to Hollywood celebrities, has been renovated into a luxury hotel and has been placed in the National Register of Historic Places.

with minimal use of exterior and interior decoration were popular. So were California developer Joseph Eichler's home designs, which featured flat and/or low-sloping A-framed roofs, vertical-patterned wood siding, and concrete slab floors. "They were important because they put modern [newly built] architecture into the hands of people who otherwise could not have afforded it,"[55] says architecture teacher Aaron Kahlenberg, whose students study Eichler's work.

Postwar Nostalgia

Restrained, understated style remained the norm until the 1960s and 1970s. By then, people were ready for brighter, more playful styles again. They also looked back on the prewar years with nostalgia and began to see art deco as an authentic artistic movement. A showcase of 1920s designs entitled Les Années 25, Art Déco/Bauhaus/Stijl/Esprit Nouveau (25 Years, Art Deco/Bauhaus/ Stijl/New Spirit), presented by the Museum of Decorative Arts in Paris in 1966, called new attention to the style. It also marked the first time the words *art deco* had ever been formally used. Weber notes, "Art deco, long scorned for its fussy ornamentalism and crass commercialism . . . was now treated as a twentieth-century design movement of respectable stature."[56]

Not only was art deco accepted as a true design style, it began to influence upcoming art and design trends. One of these trends was pop art, a 1960s style that used themes and images drawn from popular culture. Similar to art deco, pop art designers made their pieces stylized, colorful, and bold. They also made them functional. Furniture, clothing, and small household items were all made in art deco–inspired, pop art styles. The lava lamp, for instance, was sleek and playful, shaped like a rocket cone and filled with colorful moving blobs of oil in water. Short, straight dresses known as "shifts" of the mid-1960s were reminiscent of flapper styles of the 1920s. So were pieces of 1960s costume jewelry in chunky, colorful plastic and enamel designs.

Memphis style, a short-lived movement of the 1980s, drew its inspiration from art deco, too. More playful than practical, the style emphasized unconventional shapes and bright, colorful pieces. Designer Martine Bedine's Super Lamp, for instance, was made of painted metal and shaped like a half circle with colored spokes that held lightbulbs. Another example of Memphis style was Ettore Sottsass's Carlton Bookcase, a colorful conglomeration of shelves set at angles that could never hold books.

Retro Art Deco

After influencing pop art and Memphis style, art deco gained greater popularity in the 1980s as a retro style—a past style that is reinvented. Retro deco pieces have variations and are more up-to-date than earlier art deco designs, but they are enough the same to be instantly recognizable.

One of the most breathtaking architectural examples of retro deco is the MI-6 headquarters building (Secret Intelligence Service building) in London, designed by leading English architect Terry Farrell and completed in 1993. Londoners nicknamed it "Legoland" for its resemblance to the interlocking building blocks, and "Babylon on Thames" for its similarity to an ancient

The MI-6 building in London, England, is a fine example of retro art deco from the 1980s.

British architect Terry Farrell has gained worldwide fame for the combination of high-tech and modernistic styling he incorporates in his buildings. Born on May 12, 1938, he opened his own firm in London in 1980 and quickly gained attention for his use of art deco style and his sense of fun. In addition to the MI-6 building, one of his notable works is the conversion of a 1930s garage into the TV-AM headquarters. He designed the building's logo to be thick, stylized letters sticking out from the wall. The entrance is topped by a sunrise archway. Twelve large egg-cup shapes march along the roofline. All emphasize the fact that the building formerly housed the station's Breakfast Television Center.

Farrell went on to win praise for his work restoring urban buildings in declining areas. His conversions include Limehouse Studios, a former rum and banana warehouse; his own offices in North London, a former tire factory; and Tobacco Dock in London's Docklands.

In addition to his headquarters in London, Farrell opened offices in Hong Kong in 1991 and Edinburgh, Scotland, in 1992. He was knighted in 2001 for his contribution to architecture and urban design and continues to create extraordinary buildings. Jay Merrick says, "Farrell is undoubtedly Britain's most respected urban masterplanner. He reminds us that there's no meaningful future without a meaningful past—and that even the most rapid change cannot afford to jettison [throw away] previous evidence of time and place."

Jay Merrick, "There's a Place for Everything," *Independent*, November 24, 2004. www.independent.co.uk/news/uk/this-britain/theres-a-place-for-everything-534339.html.

Babylonian ziggurat (a temple in the form of a terraced tower). Its pyramid shape, streamlined starkness, and the zigzag effect created by its windows make it classic art deco, however.

Retro deco has continued in popularity into the twenty-first century. Today, it can be recognized on buildings, on stylized magazine covers, and in furniture and accessories. The Parkview Square office building in Singapore, built in 2002,

"FASHION IS CYCLICAL, DARLING"

The twenty-first century saw renewed interest in 1920s and 1930s styles of clothing and jewelry. Fashionistas Sarah-Louise Boyd and Joanne Bennett give details in an article titled "Designers Revisit Depression Era Chic."

Fashion is cyclical, darling, and for the upcoming fall/winter lines, the 1930s are what's en vogue [in style]. . . . Many of today's top designers are finding inspiration in the fluid forms of the 1930s for their . . . collections. Spring and summer saw the resurgence of the light chiffons and subdued floral prints popular during the Depression era. For fall, expect to see more true feminine glamour, with flowing fabrics, tiers of ruffles, and luxurious ropes of pearls in the ready-to-wear lines of names like John Galliano and Baby Phat.

To keep things modern, the romantic, girly looks may be a bit edgier for fall. Art deco–inspired accessories, such as rhinestone jewelry and intricate lace handbags, also will be all the rage. So, keep your eye out for these 1930s styles, whether vintage or new, as the fashion industry makes new strides along the catwalk of history."

Sarah-Louise Boyd and Joanne Bennett, "Designers Revisit Depression Era Chic," Retro Radar.com, 2008. hwww.retroradar.com/1930s-fashion-revival.

Shown here is an art deco onyx and diamond necklace by Cartier.

Stars often borrow their vintage art deco jewelry, but it can be purchased from jewelers like Harry Winston, who began designing and collecting jewelry as early as the 1920s. Two twenty-first-century jewelry designers, Carl Blackburn and Cathy Heinz, are known for their retro deco necklaces, earrings, and other pieces made with platinum, diamonds, gold, and pearls. Heinz's work is more casual and playful, while Blackburn's is elegant and includes filigree (lacy-looking) patterns and geometric designs. Blackburn's engagement rings are unusual in that he uses a deco practice of mixing colored stones with diamonds to help create his vintage effect.

In addition to purchasing art deco engagement rings, many women are having art deco weddings, in which everything from invitations to the vintage car that carries them away from the church is representative of the style. Dresses are "flapper style" with low waists, slim silhouettes, and beaded decoration. Jazz is played at the reception, while the wedding cake is created in zigzag moderne or streamline moderne design. Ceremonies and receptions are even held in historic or retro art deco buildings, such as art deco movie theaters.

Preserving Deco

During the time when art deco was not recognized or appreciated as a style, many art deco venues such as movie theaters were torn down to make way for more up-to-date homes and businesses. Other vintage pieces were lost, too. Clothing wore out. Glassware was broken.

When art deco lovers recognized that irreplaceable things—particularly buildings—were being destroyed, they came together to preserve those that were left. The first of such groups was the Miami Design Preservation League (MDPL), founded in 1976. Led by founder Barbara Baer Capitman, league members fought bulldozers and demolition crews that were beginning to knock down many Miami Beach art deco buildings that were no longer considered attractive. "She would push and agitate and cause trouble until people wouldn't speak to her," said Michael Kinerk, another founding member of the League. "She was interested in results, not social sensitivities."[58]

Tourists and residents attend the Miami Design Preservation League's annual Art Deco Week festival that raises awareness and appreciation of Miami's art deco district.

Due to the league's efforts, in 1979 the South Beach art deco district was recognized as historic by the U.S. government, and demolition stopped. The historic designation also drew attention from those who appreciated the style and were willing to invest in it. With new owners, new paint, and new purpose, more than seven hundred art deco buildings were saved and restored. One of these buildings is the Essex House Hotel, designed by Henry Hohauser and built in 1938. Streamlined, flat-roofed, and studded with porthole windows, it resembles a land-bound ocean liner. Another is the Marlin Hotel, notable for its streamlined corners and undersea motifs above its front entrance. The Marlin was designed by L. Murray Dixon, who designed hundreds of art deco hotels, apartment houses, stores, and residences in the 1930s and 1940s in

Miami. David Vela, regional director for the U.S. Department of the Interior's National Park Service (the agency that oversees the National Register of Historic Places), says, "Miami Beach's Art Deco District is a living museum teeming with a vibrant residential population, businesses, tourism and entertainment. . . . It is a testament to how preservation can benefit our communities."[59]

Other Preservation Groups

The Miami Design Preservation League was not alone in its efforts. Various other preservation societies arose over time as well. Today, active groups in the United States range from New York City to Seattle, Washington. The Chicago Art Deco Society, for instance, works to protect everything from high-rise structures like the Daily News Building to smaller public buildings that are being lost from Chicago neighborhoods. In Los Angeles, the Art Deco Society does the same, focusing particularly on classic movie theaters that are in danger of being demolished. The Los Angeles Conservancy, another preservation society, is the largest membership-based historic preservation organization in the United States.

Preservation groups have sprung up in other parts of the world, too. The Thirties Society (now the Twentieth Century Society) was formed in Great Britain in 1979 in an effort to gain protection for British buildings built between World War I and World War II. The society's first real challenge was a movement to save the Firestone Factory on the Great West Road out of London. Despite many efforts, it was torn down in August 1980. Because of its loss, however, the society was able to draw public attention to the necessity of preserving other buildings. They have succeeded in getting the government to protect over 150 examples of 1920s and 1930s architecture over time.

The Art Deco Trust

Another notable preservation group outside the United States is the Art Deco Trust in Napier, New Zealand. Formed in 1985, the trust aims to protect the many art deco buildings that celebrate a catastrophic yet courageous period in the town's history.

Napier was just another small coastal village when, on February 3, 1931, a 7.8 magnitude earthquake struck, toppling buildings, sparking fires, and leaving the town in ruins. With residents left homeless, a reconstruction committee was formed and four regional architects were commissioned to get the town rebuilt. They rushed to complete the task, and as a result, virtually all buildings were designed in a style that was modern at the time—art deco. Tinniswood notes:

> Interestingly, the presence of so much art deco in Napier . . . owed less to the influence of any one architect than to post-earthquake practicalities. In the aftermath of the disaster, simple reinforced-concrete box construction was considered the most sensible option, because concrete buildings were quick and easy to produce and had stood up to the earthquake better than anything else.[60]

Today, the trust reaches out to neighboring towns to encourage them to preserve their art deco structures. It also works to draw attention to the importance of the style. Due to its efforts, Napier is known worldwide for its art deco and is one of the most photographed tourist destinations in New Zealand.

Need to Preserve

Although art deco is recognized and respected in many countries of the world, more effort is needed to preserve its unique architectural designs, especially in developing countries where funds are scarce. One of these places is Mumbai (formerly Bombay), India, where many art deco buildings are being demolished to make way for newer, high-occupancy buildings.

Unknown to most, Mumbai has one of the largest collections of art deco architecture in the world. Two areas of the city where it can be seen are the Oval Maidan and Marine Drive districts. There, homes display the style inside and out. Although some are dirty and falling into disrepair, art

deco moldings and bronze and stainless steel fittings are everywhere. On public buildings, ornamental sculptures depict an Indian influence. The Mumbai Heritage Conservation Committee was formed in 1995 to press for government protection for the districts, but thus far, that protection has not been adequate. Conservationist and historian Sharada Dwivedi states: "The need of the hour is to create more awareness among . . . the citizens, so that they actively participate in the conservation movement. More powers should be given to locally-constituted bodies like the Mumbai Heritage Conservation Committee (MHCC), which is merely an advisory body without any punitive powers, like a tiger without teeth."[61]

Another city in danger of losing its art deco treasures is Shanghai, China. In the 1930s the city experienced an economic boom, and city leaders wanted new construction to be as up-to-date as possible. Thus, office buildings, apartment houses, and large homes were built in art deco style. The Langham Yangtze Boutique Hotel (formerly the Yangtze Hotel) and Eddington House are two of the few that have been restored. Many of the

The recently renovated lobby of the Peace Hotel in Shanghai, China, boasts a beautiful art deco style. The hotel is a part of the effort to retain Shanghai's art deco–style buildings.

Wimbledon Titles, Dies at 92," *New York Times*, January 3, 1998, p. D16.

15. Quoted in Herbert Hoover Presidential Library and Museum, "Frequently Asked Questions," 2010. http://hoover.archives.gov/info/faq.html#chicken.

16. Quoted in Robert S. Lynd and Helen Merrell Lynd, *Middletown: A Study in Contemporary American Culture*. New York: Harcourt Brace, 1929, p. 46.

17. Quoted in AdClassic.com, "1920 Columbia Grafanola Ad," 2010. www.adclassix.com/ads/20columbia grafonola.htm.

18. Quoted in PBS.com, "Early Jazz; 1920-1930," 2010. www.pbs.org/wgbh/cultureshock/flashpoints/music/jazz.html.

19. Klein et al., McClelland, and Haslam, *In the Deco Style*, p. 167.

Chapter 2: Sunbursts, Zigzags, and Color

20. Quoted in Rich East High School Website, "Art Deco, 1925–1940."

21. Quoted in Robert W. Rydell, *World of Fairs: The Century of Progress Expositions*. Chicago: University of Chicago Press, 1993, p. 73.

22. Quoted in Bevis Hillier and Stephen Escritt, *Art Deco Style*. London: Phaidon, 1997, p. 28.

23. Quoted in Hillier and Escritt, *Art Deco Style*, p. 59.

24. Quoted in Diner Man, "1943 Jerry O'Mahony Dining Cars Ad," 2009. http://dinerman.wordpress.com/2009/02/24/jerry-omahony-dining-cars.

25. Robert Fulford, "Art Deco's Glamour," *National Post*, September 2003. www.robertfulford.com/2003-09-13-deco.html.

26. Quoted in Architonic, "'Beta' Chair: Sotheby's," 1934. www.architonic.com/dcsht/beta-chair-sothebys/4107744.

27. Quoted in Adrian Tinniswood, *The Art Deco House*. New York: Watson-Guptill, 2002, p. 49.

28. Quoted in Anthony Alofsin, *Frank Lloyd Wright: The Lost Years, 1910–1922*. Chicago: University of Chicago Press, 1993, p. 221.

29. Eva Weber, *American Art Deco*. North Dighton, MA: World Publications, 2005, p. 7.

30. Tinniswood, *The Art Deco House*, p. 93.

31. Fakelite.com, "What Is Bakelite?" 2004. www.fakelite.com/bakelite.htm.

32. Hiller and Escritt, *Art Deco Style*, p. 24.

Chapter 3: Deco and the Department Store

33. Quoted in Retropolis, "Virtual Visit to the 1925 Paris Exposition des Art Decoratifs," 2006. www.retropolis.net/exposition/aftermath.html.

34. Quoted in John Tauranac, *The Empire State Building: The Making of a Landmark*. New York: Scribner, 1995, p. 150.

35. Quoted in Lucy Fischer, *Designing Women: Cinema, Art Deco, and the Female Form*. New York: Columbia University Press, 2003, p. 47.
36. Quoted in Fischer, *Designing Women*, p. 72.
37. Quoted in Fischer, *Designing Women*, p. 71.
38. Gaston, *Collector's Guide to Art Deco*, p. 12.
39. Quoted in Michael D. Kinerk and Dennis W. Wilhelm, *Popcorn Palaces: The Art Deco Movie Theatre Paintings of Davis Cone*. New York: Harry N. Abrams, 2001, p. 6.
40. Quoted in Collectics, "Fiesta, Fiestaware & Homer Laughlin China Company," 1998. www.collectics.com/education_fiesta.html.

Chapter 4: Architectural Modernism

41. Tauranac, *The Empire State Building*, p. 146.
42. Anindita Dasgupta, "Museum Acquires Thousands of Ocean Liner Artifacts," Downtown Express, August 18–24, 2006. www.downtownexpress.com/de_171/museumacquires.html.
43. *Literary Digest*, "1927 Description of the New French Ocean Liner Ile de France," July 16, 1927. www.1920-30.com/travel/ile-de-france.html.
44. Quoted in Eric C. Rodenberg, "Sailing the SS Normandie," Antique Week.com, February 12, 2010. http://antiquewest.net/ArchiveArticle.asp?newsid=1531.
45. Tauranac, *The Empire State Building*, p. 152.
46. Quoted in Bruce Brooks Pfeiffer and Gerald Nordland, eds., *Frank Lloyd Wright: In the Realm of Ideas*. Carbondale: Southern Illinois University Press, 1987, p. 15.
47. Eric P. Nash, *Manhattan Skyscrapers*. New York: Princeton Architectural Press, 1995, p. 55.
48. Quoted in David Garrard Lowe, "The Triumph of Rockefeller Center," *City Journal*, Summer 1995. www.city-journal.org/html/5_3_a2.html.
49. Eva Weber, *Art Deco*. North Dighton, MA: World Publications, 2003, p. 85.
50. Tinniswood, *The Art Deco House*, p. 114.
51. Quoted in Sharon Bond, "St. Petersburg Store's Cloud Furniture Line Echoes Art Deco Design," *St. Petersburg Times*, February 14, 2009. www.tampabay.com/features/homeandgarden/article975446.ece.
52. Quoted in Fischer, *Designing Women*, pp. 109–11.
53. Quoted in Fischer, *Designing Women*, p. 201.

Chapter 5: Deco Revival

54. Stanley K. Schultz, "World War II, the Impact at Home," American History 102, 1999. http://us.history.wisc.edu/hist102/lectures/lecture21.html.
55. Quoted in Dana Bartholomew, "Preserving Eichler's Valley Homes," *Los Angeles Daily News*, February 12,

2010. www.dailynews.com/news/ci_
14386819.

56. Weber, *American Art Deco*, p. 14.

57. Quoted in Kim Cook, "Art Deco Furniture Has a Revival," *Wilkes-Barre* (PA) *Times Leader*, January 10, 2009. www.timesleader.com/features/homegarden/Art_Deco_furniture_has_a_revival_01-09-2009.html.

58. Quoted in Joan Cook, "Barbara Baer Capitman, 69, Dies; Created Miami Art Deco District," *New York Times*, March 31, 1990, p. 12.

59. Quoted in Jose Lima, "Miami Beach Celebrates 30th Anniversary of Art Deco District Designation on National Register of Historic Places,"
Preservation Directory.com, May 26, 2009. www.preservationdirectory.com/PreservationBlogs/ArticleDetail.aspx?id=1099&catid=11.

60. Tinniswood, *The Art Deco House*, p. 99.

61. Quoted in Harpreet Kaur, "A Call for Conservation," Dance with Shadows, July 16, 2004. www.dancewithshadows.com/mumbai_architecture_heritage.asp.

62. Quoted in Gary Jones, "Saving Grace," *Time International*, March 5, 2007, p. 46.

63. Quoted in Kati Turcu, "Art Deco for All," *Epoch Times*, July 11, 2008. www.theepochtimes.com/news/8-7-11/73320.html.

Glossary

art nouveau: A style of fine and applied art of the late nineteenth and early twentieth centuries. It is characterized chiefly by curved lines and natural forms.

avant-garde: Unorthodox, daring, advanced.

champlevé: An enameling technique in which enamel is fused onto the hollowed areas of a metal piece.

chryselephantine: Made of metal and ivory; an ancient Greek technique of making statues and figurines by bonding ivory and gold together.

cubism: A painting and sculpture style developed in Paris in the early twentieth century. It is characterized by the reduction and fragmentation of natural forms into abstract, geometric structures.

frieze: Decorative band on an outside wall bearing lettering, sculpture, etc.

marquetry: Material such as wood or ivory set into a wood surface in an intricate design.

modernistic: A term used to describe art deco style, emphasizing the departure from previous artistic styles.

motif: A form or image that is repeatedly used.

mullion: A vertical structure of stone, wood, or some other material that divides windows or some other opening.

neoclassicism: A primarily European and American architectural movement that was fashionable during the late eighteenth and early nineteenth centuries. It is characterized by the use of Greek or Roman decorative motifs, a focus on simple, geometric arrangements, the use of light colors, shallowness of sculptural details on facades, and the avoidance of textural effects.

opalescent: Exhibiting a play of colors like that of an opal.

pediment: A triangular-shaped area below the roofline on the end wall of a building.

shagreen: Shark or stingray skin processed to look like leather.

spandrel: A panel-like area between the head of a window on one level and the sill of a window immediately above.

streamline: The design of a smooth object shaped so that its drag is reduced as it moves through air or water.

style moderne: Art deco style.

stylize: To portray in a nonrealistic way. Art deco stylization uses simplified figures that give off a feeling of movement, energy, and athleticism.

For More Information

Books

Richard Berenholtz, *New York Deco*. New York: Welcome Books, 2009. An overview of well-known and lesser-known art deco buildings in New York City.

Barbara Baer Capitman, Michael D. Kinerk, and Dennis W. Wilhelm, *Rediscovering Art Deco USA*. New York: Viking, 1994. A survey of the United States' art deco architectural heritage.

Bruce LaFontaine, *Famous Buildings of Frank Lloyd Wright*. Mineola, NY: Dover, 1997. Illustrations of forty-four structures designed by one of the twentieth century's most influential architects.

Katharine Morrison McClinton, *Introduction to Lalique Glass*. Des Moines: Wallace-Homestead, 1978. Provides an overview of artist René Lalique's glasswork.

Mike Schafer and Joe Welsh, *Streamliners: History of a Railroad Icon*. St. Paul, MN: MBI, 2002. A history of streamlined trains in the United States through the years. Great photos.

Websites

Decodame.com (www.decodame.com/index.html). The website offers a chance to view and purchase new and vintage art deco furniture, lighting, jewelry, and art.

The Normandie (www.alae.us/Normandie). A history and virtual tour of the 1930s oceanliner.

Retropolis.net (www.retropolis.net). A website directory of art deco antiques, furniture, jewelry, and interior designers.

The Roaring Twenties (www.1920-30.com). Gives information about many aspects of the 1920s and 1930s, including politics, health practices, travel, and art deco style.

Index

Empire State Building (New York
    City), 8, 12, 13, *13*, 14, 41, 75
Enamel, 56
Erh, Deke, 96
Escritt, Stephen, 47
Essex House Hotel (Miami), 92
Etling, Edmond, 60
Expert, Roger-Henri, 70
Exposition Internationale des Arts
    Décoratifs et Industriels Modernes
    (Paris, 1925), 32–34

F
Factory of Sèvers pavilion, *33*
Farrell, Terry, 86, 87
Faulkner, Ann Shaw, 26
Fauvism, 39
Federal Art Project, 30
Fiestaware, 59
Finn, Robin, 23
Firestone Factory (London), 93
Fitzgerald, F. Scott, 19
Flappers, 21
Ford, Henry, 21
Frank, Michael, 56
Fulford, Robert, 36
Futurism, 39

G
Galeries Lafayette department store
    (Paris), 17, *17*
Gallagher, Fiona, 15
Gaston, Mary Frank, 15
Genauer, Emily, 34
Germany, rise of Third Reich in, 30

Gibbons, Cedric, 42
Glassware, 60–63
Golden Gate Bridge, 72, *72*
Good Housekeeping (magazine), 52
    Ford Motor Company ad in, *53*
Gould, Grace Margaret, 22
Goulden, Jean, 57, 59
Goupy, Marcel, 60
Grange, Red, 23
Grasset, Eugéne, 32
Gray, Christopher, 57
Great Depression, 28–30
Guimard, Hector, 32

H
Hammond, Aubrey, 50
Harbeson, John, 67
Harding, Warren G., 18
Harlem Renaissance, 26
Heinz, Cathy, 91
Hewlett, J. Monroe, 49
Hillier, Bevis, 32, 47
Hitler, Adolf, 30
Hohauser, Henry, 92
Hollyhock House (Los Angeles),
    41
Hollywood, golden age of,
    30–31
Hollywood deco, 81–82
Hood, Raymond, 75
Hoover, Herbert, 25
Horwitt, Nathan George, 39
Hughes, Howard, 84
Hughes, Langston, 26
Hurten, Frederick, 59

Picture Credits

About the Author

Diane Yancey lives in the Pacific Northwest with her husband, Michael, and their cats, Newton, Lily, and Alice. She has written more than twenty-five books for middle-grade and high school readers, including the *Life During the Roaring Twenties*, *Life During the Dust Bowl*, *Al Capone*, and *Al Capone's Chicago*.